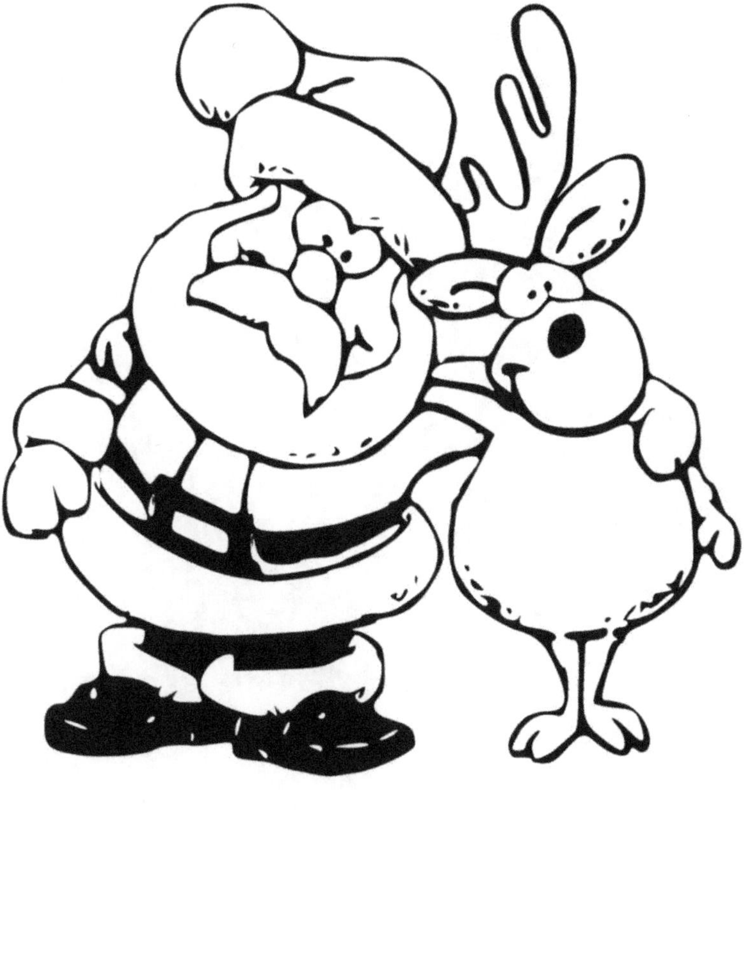

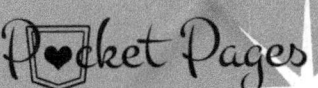

Christmas Coloring Book

Perfect Stocking Stuffer

FOR ADULTS

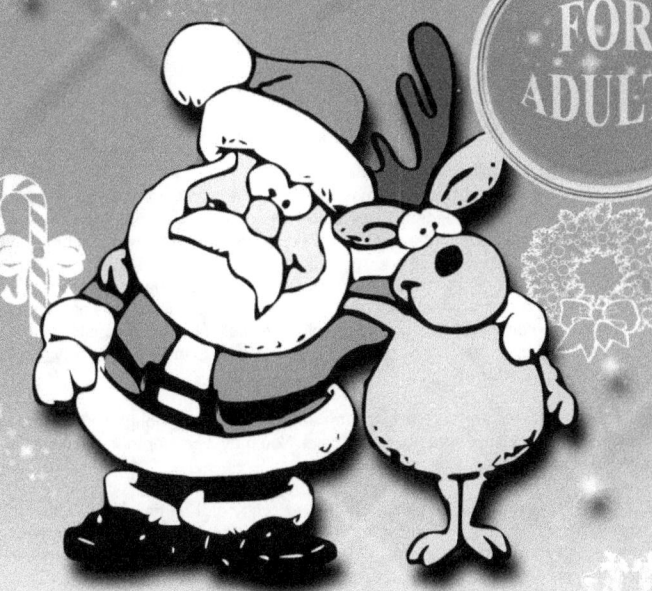

Holiday Edition

Copyright © 2020 by T. Irvolino
All rights reserved. No part of this book may be used or reproduced or transmitted in any form or by any means, electronic or mechanical including photocopying, recording, or by any information storage or retrieval system without express written permission from the publisher.

The information provided within this Book is for general informational purposes only. While we try to keep the information up-to-date and correct, there are no representations or warranties, express or implied, about the completeness, accuracy, reliability, suitability or availability with respect to the information, products, services, or related graphics contained in this Book for any purpose. Any use of this information is at your own risk.

The methods describe within this Book are the author's personal thoughts. They are not intended to be a definitive set of instructions for this project. You may discover there are other methods and materials to accomplish the same end result.

The author has made every effort to ensure the accuracy of the information within this book was correct at time of publication. The author and publisher do not assume and hereby disclaims any liability to any party for any loss, damage, or disruption caused by errors or omissions, whether such errors or omissions result from accident, negligence, or any other cause.

Attributes: Brusheezy.com

Sun Media Group, LLC
First Book Publication Date: 10/2020
Cover Illustration: T. Irvolino
To contact Author, please email publisher: sunmediagroupllc@gmail.com

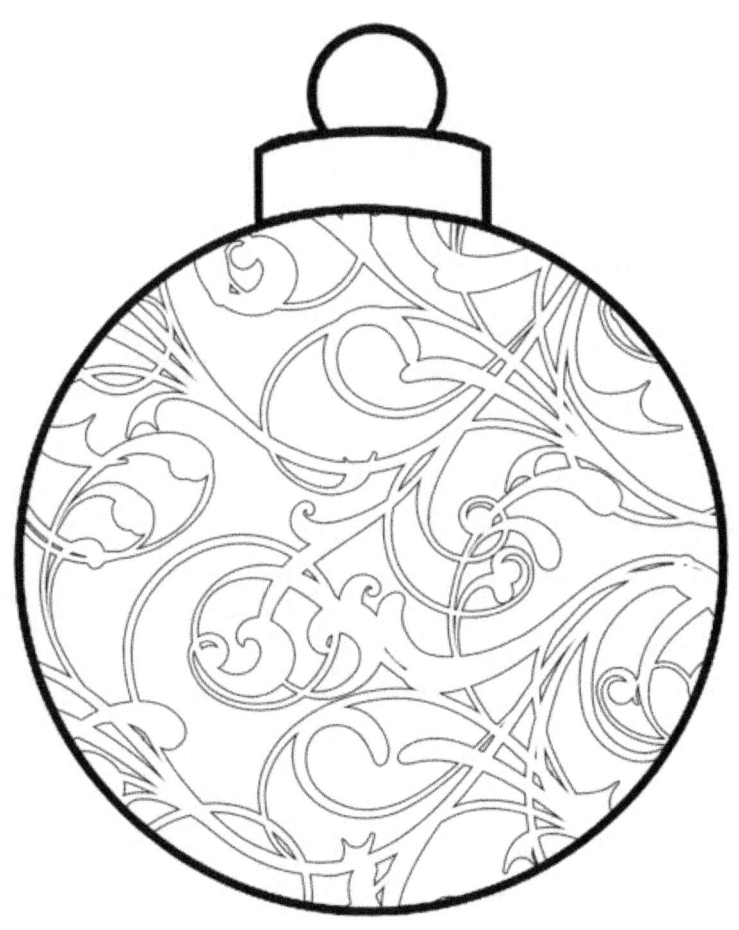

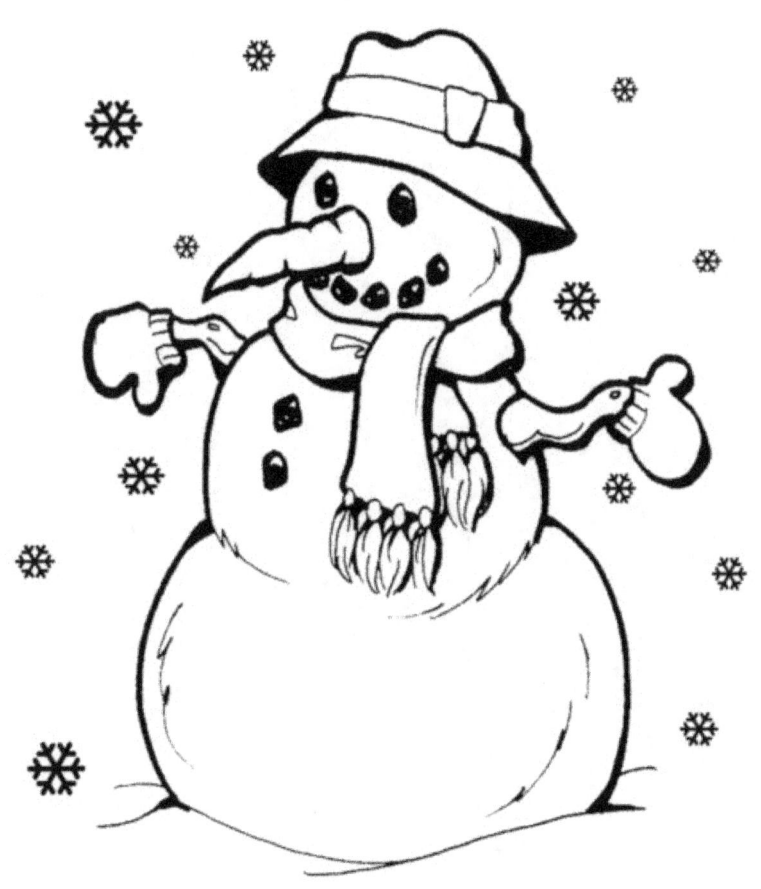

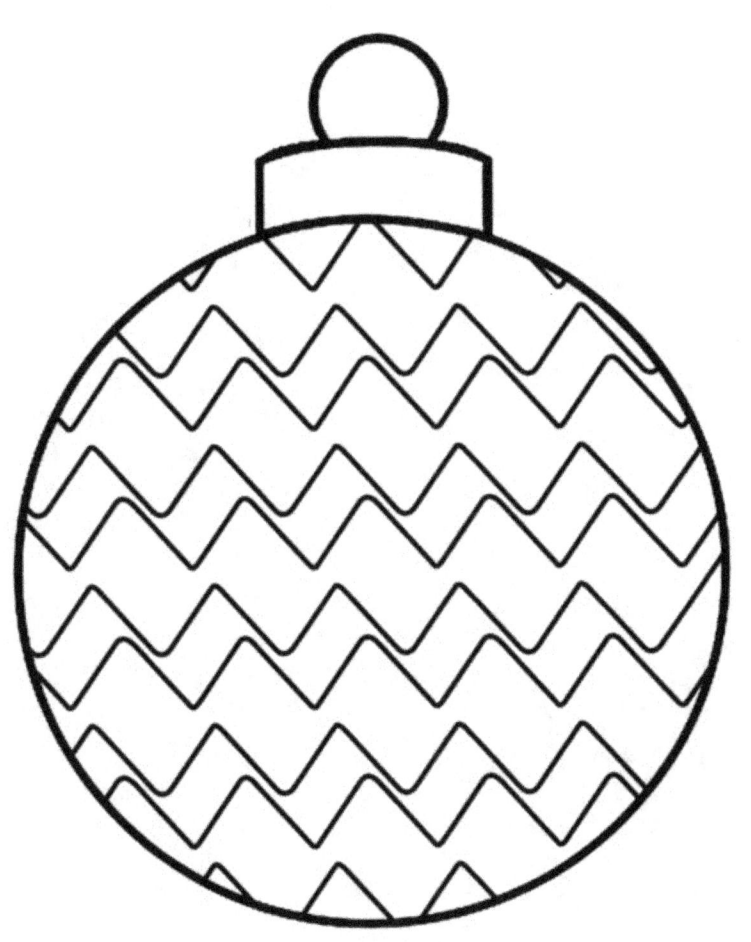

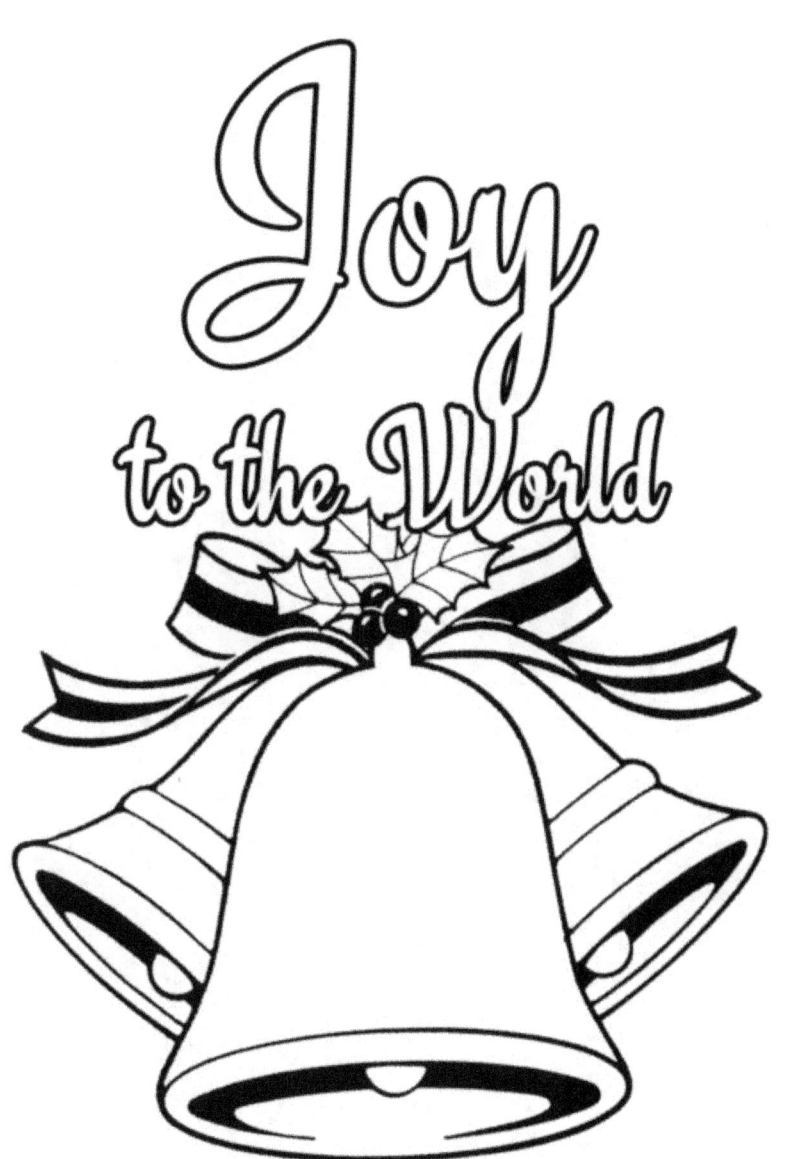

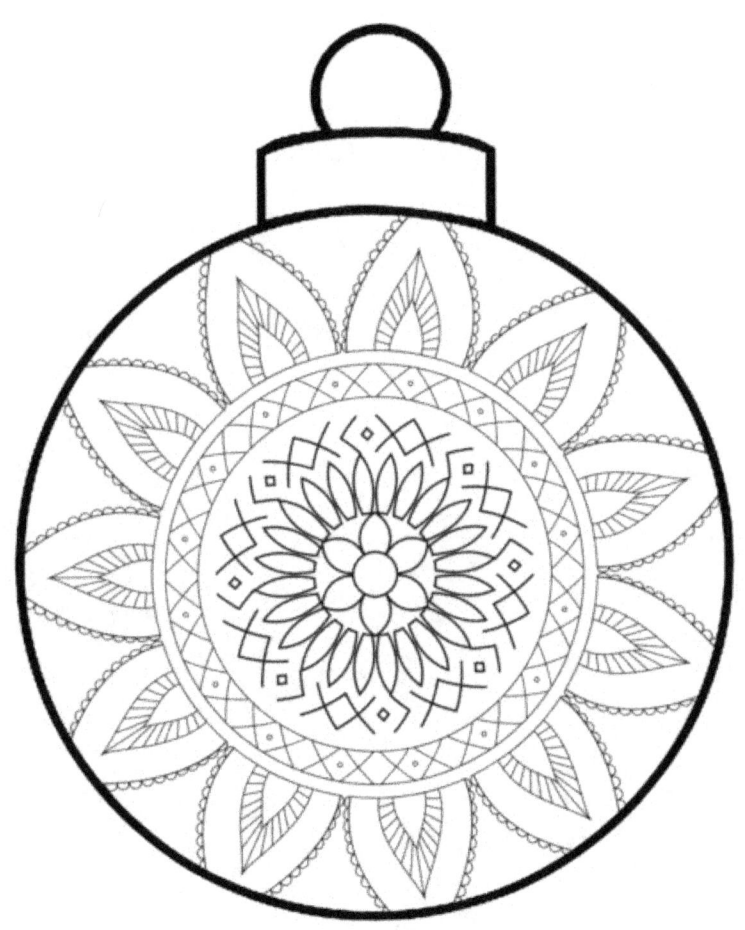

Dasher

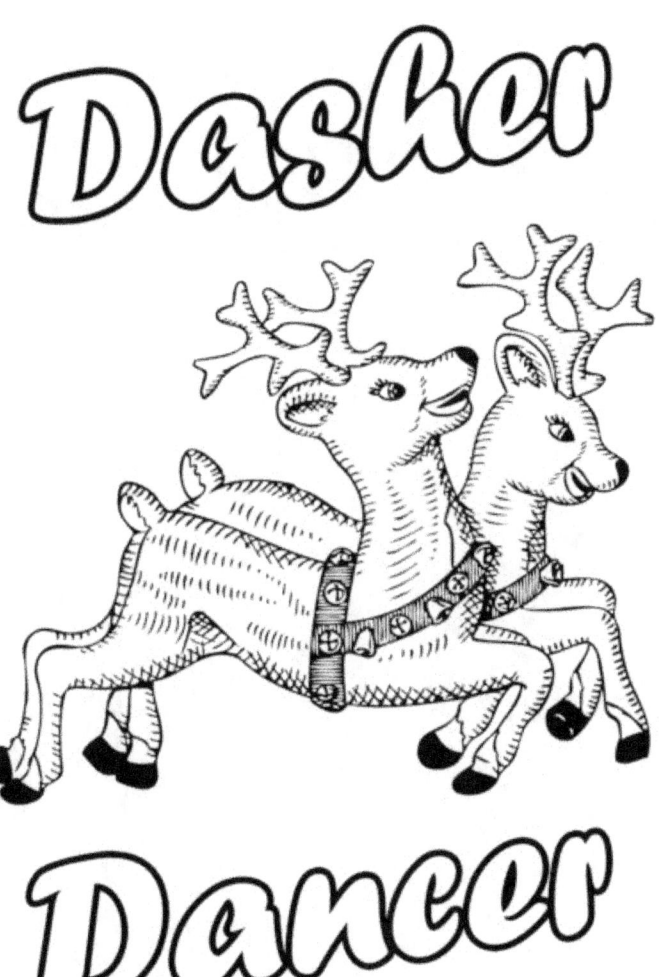

Dancer

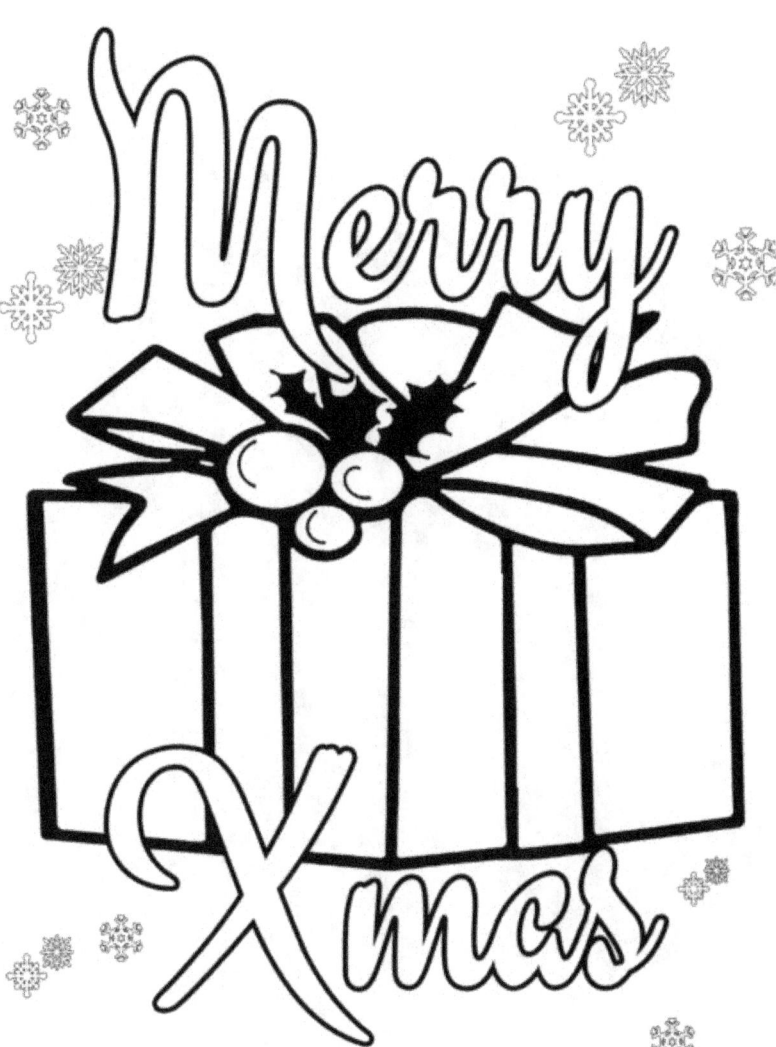

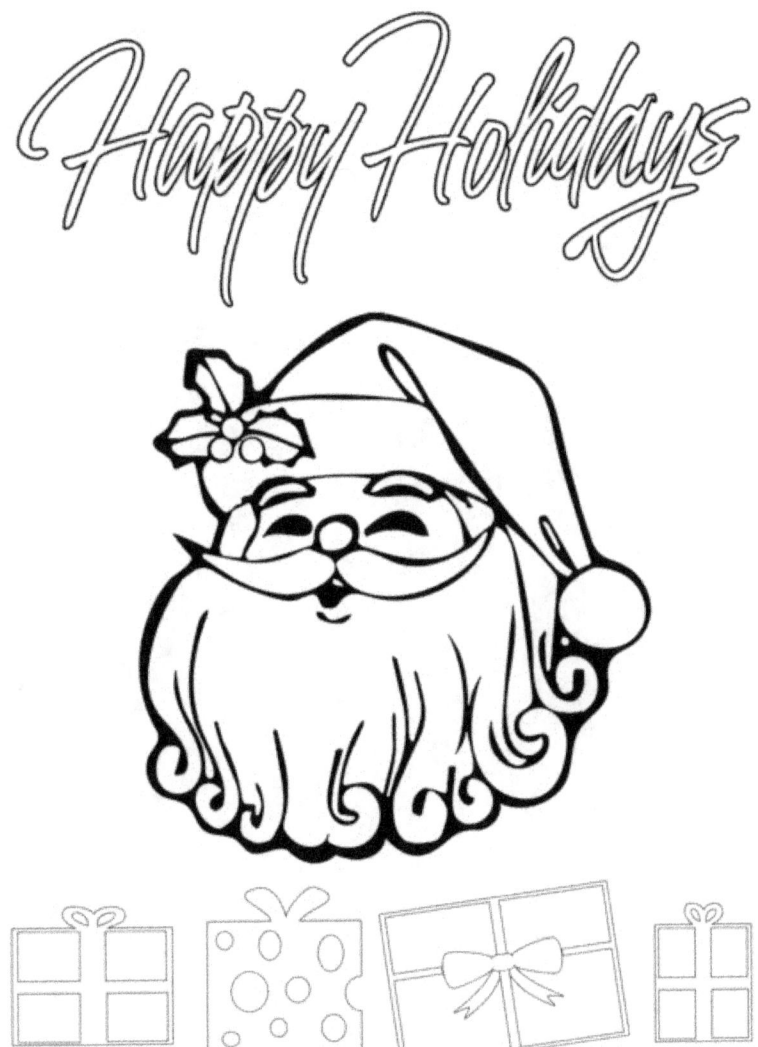

Pocket Pages

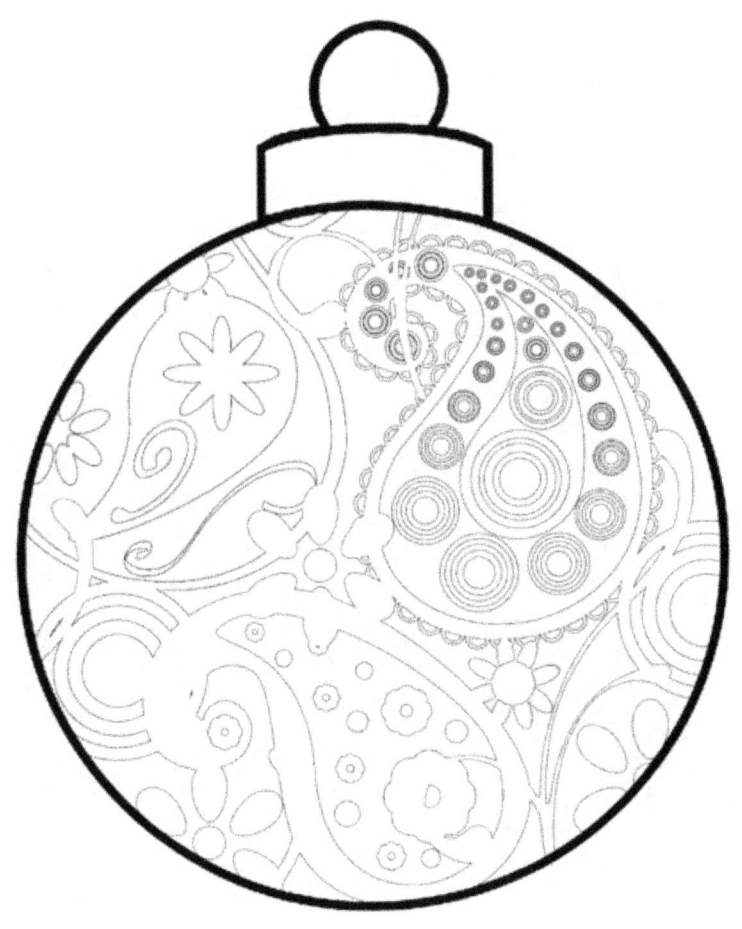

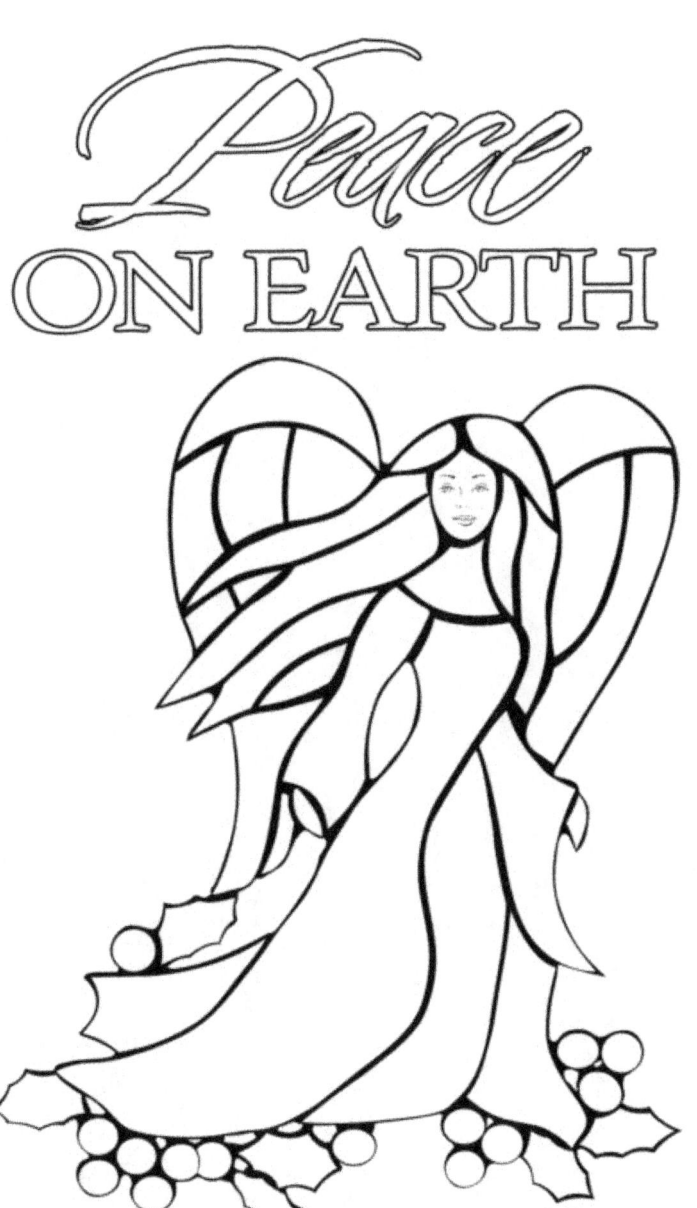

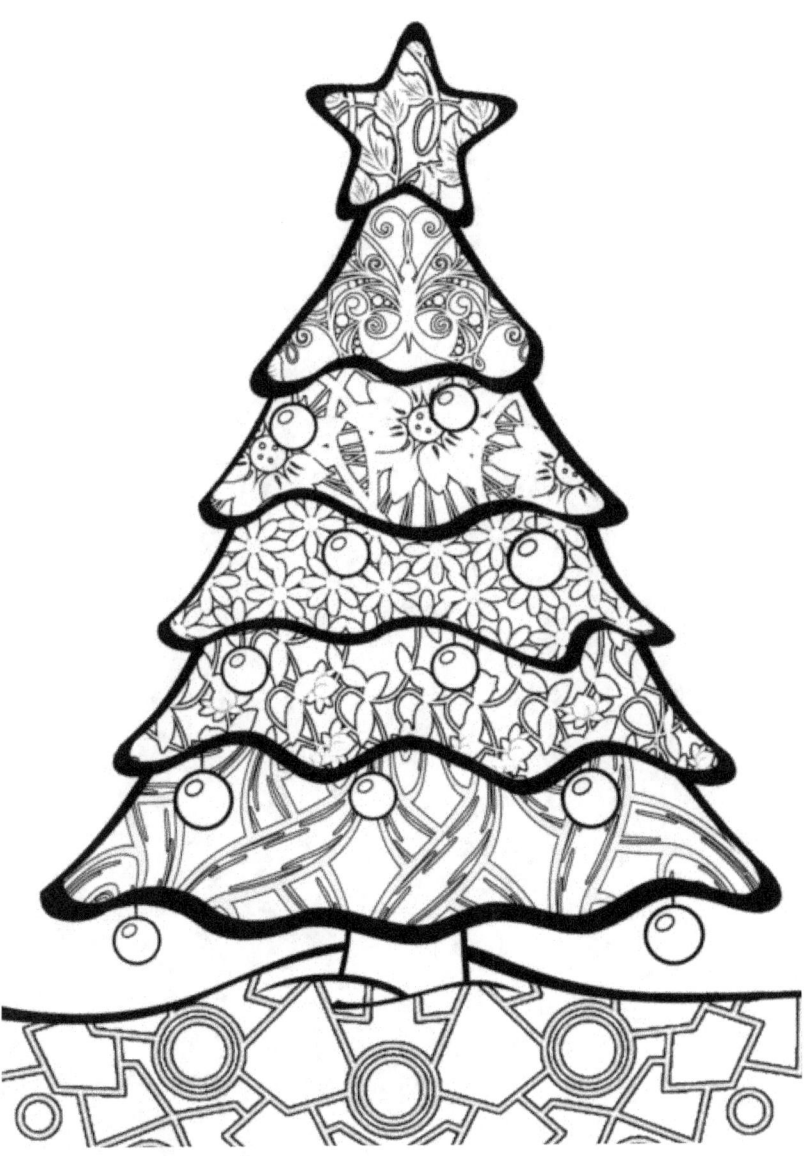

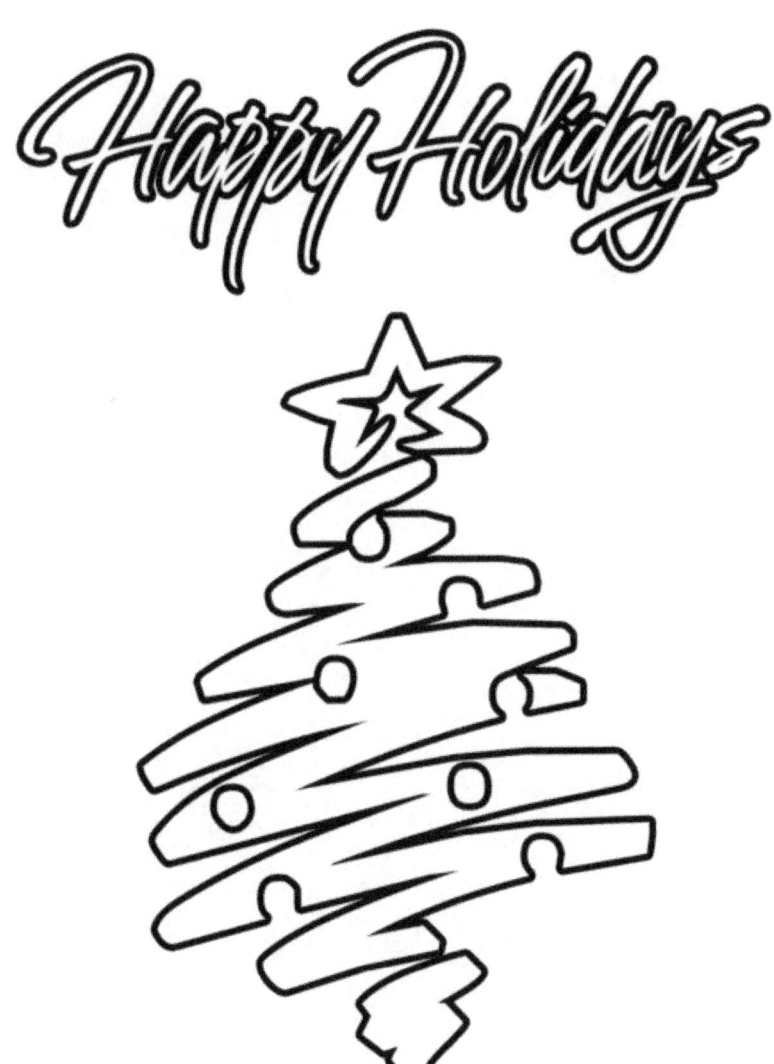

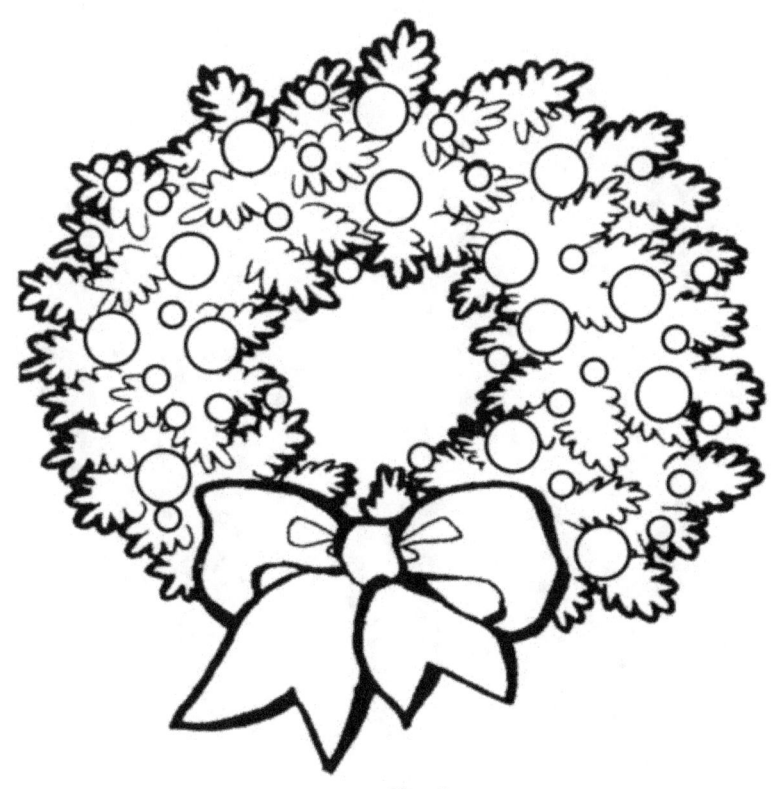

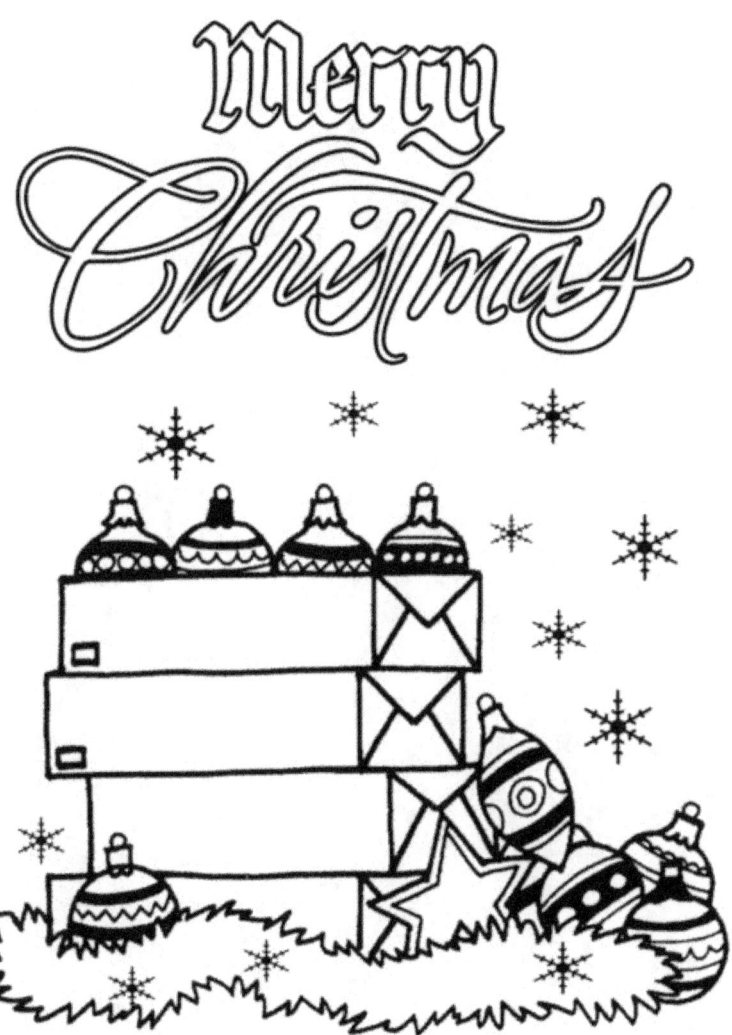

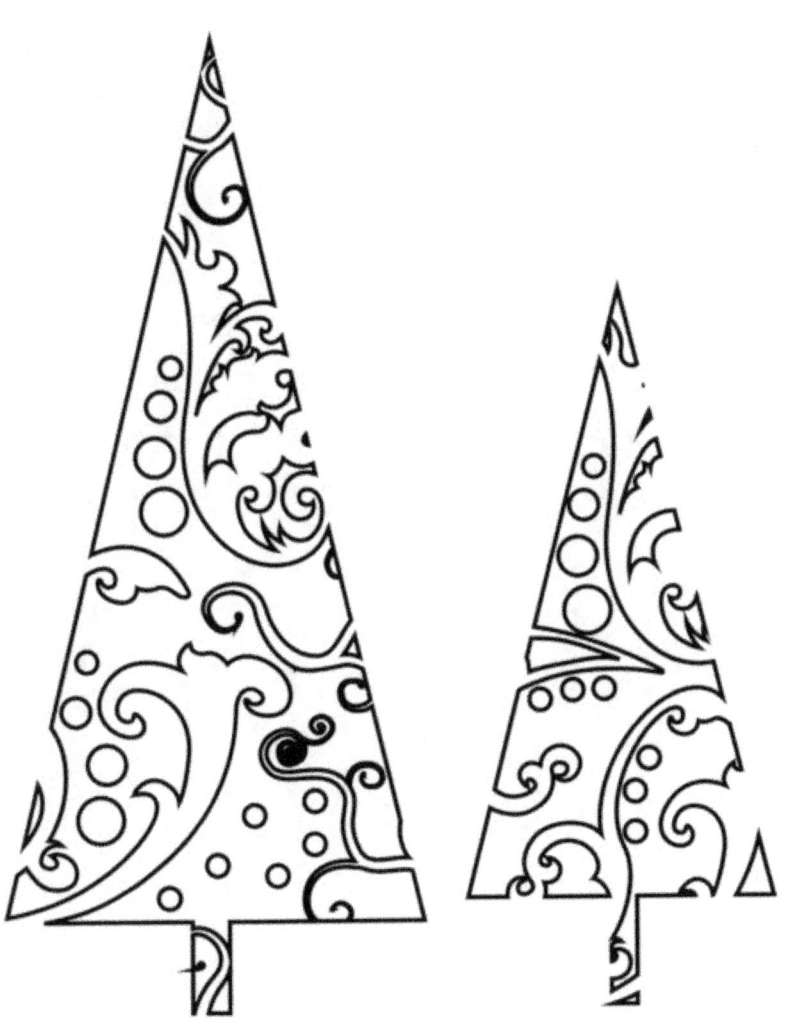

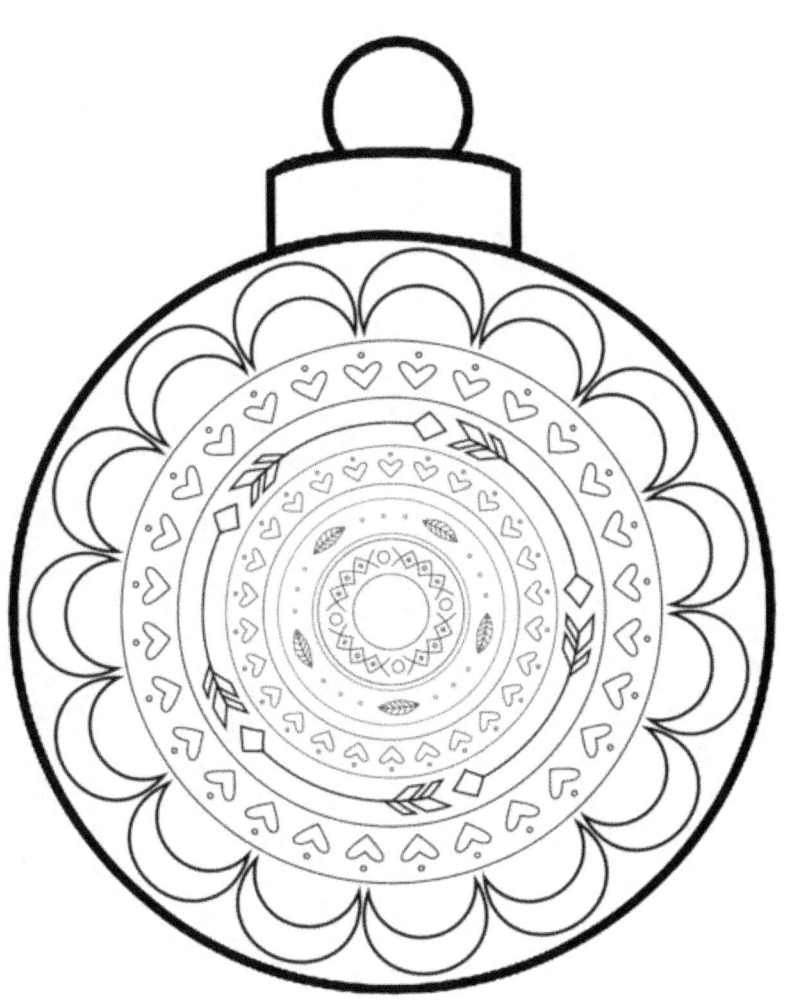

Pocket Pages

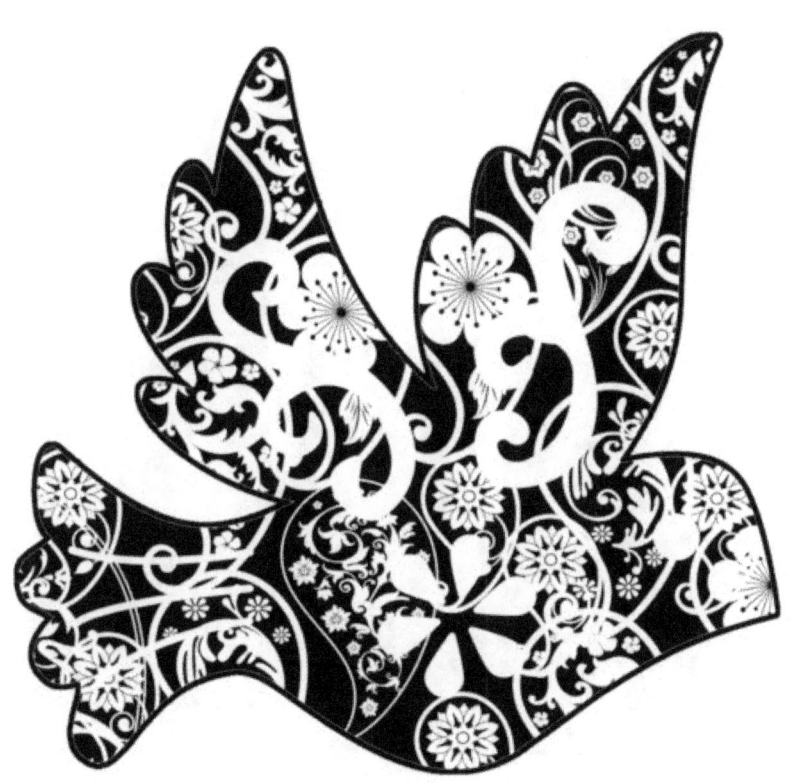

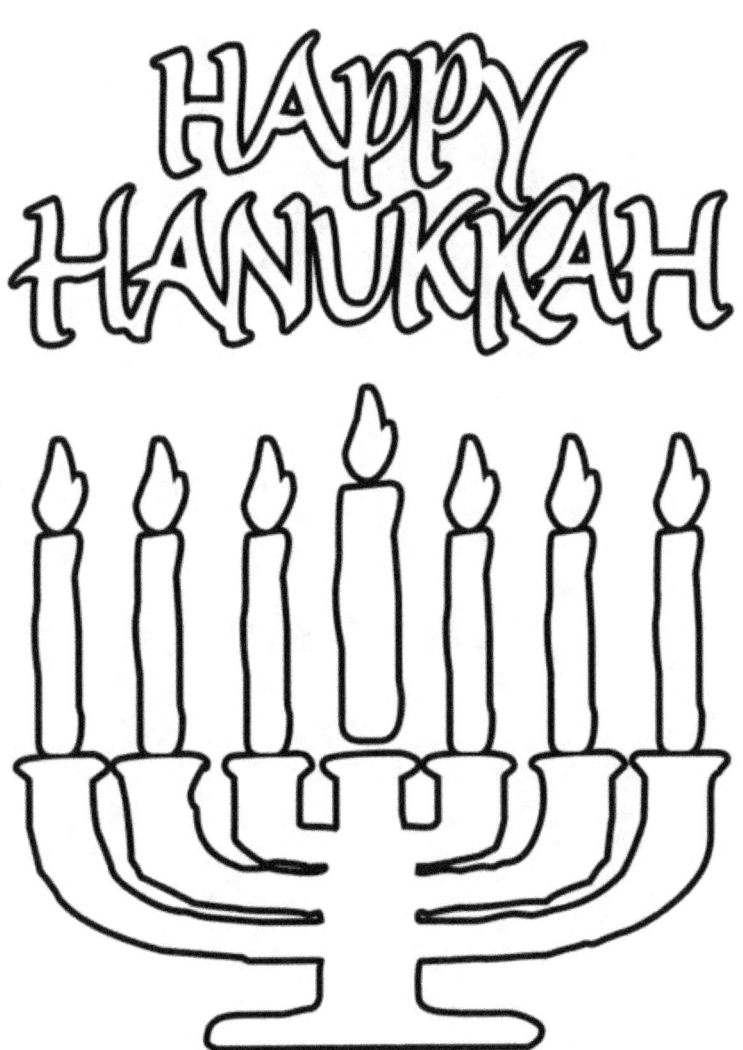

Pocket Pages

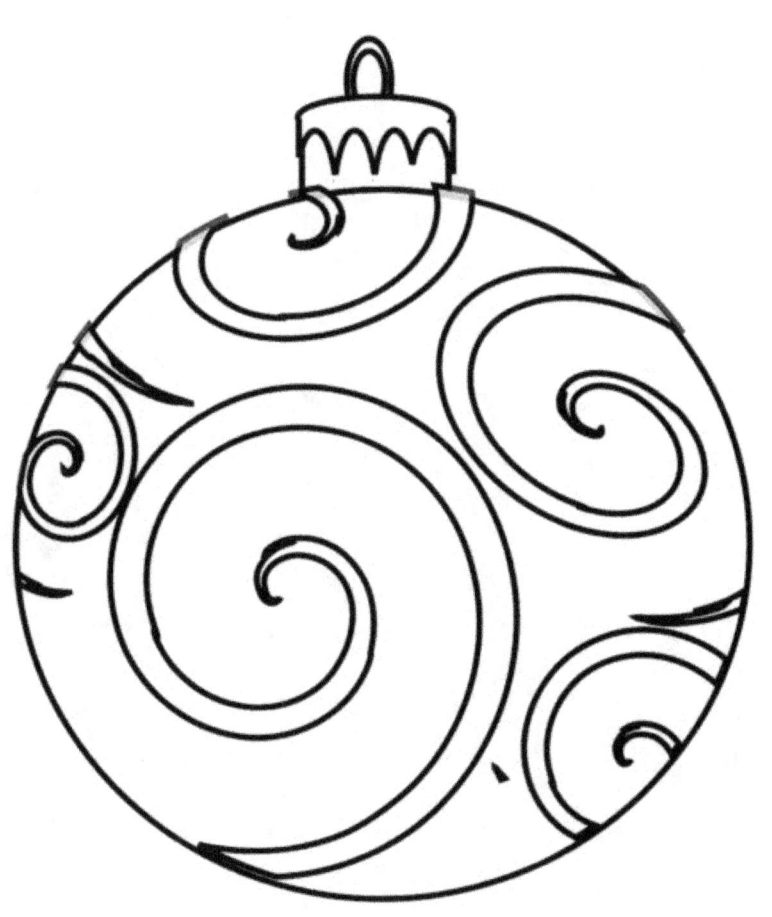

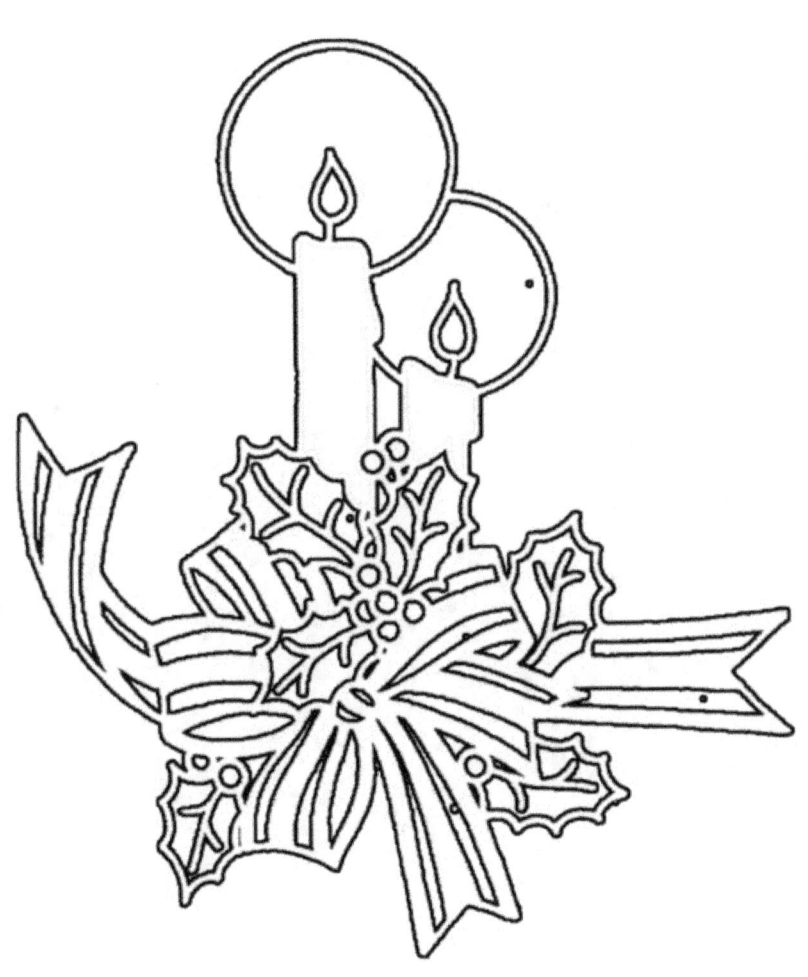

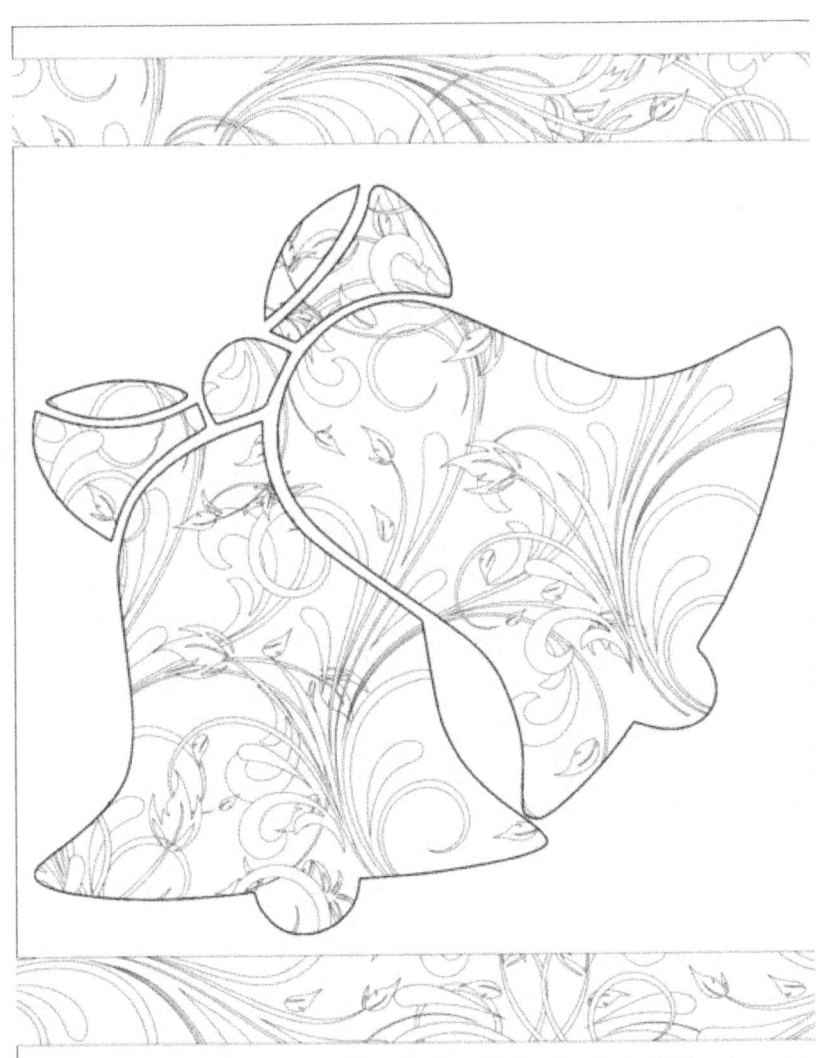

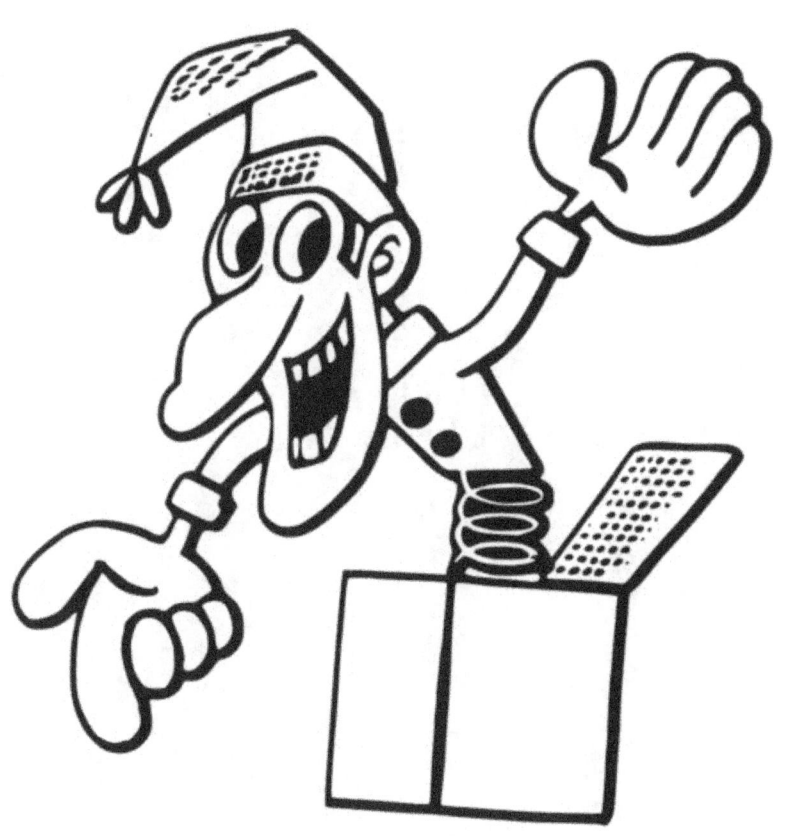

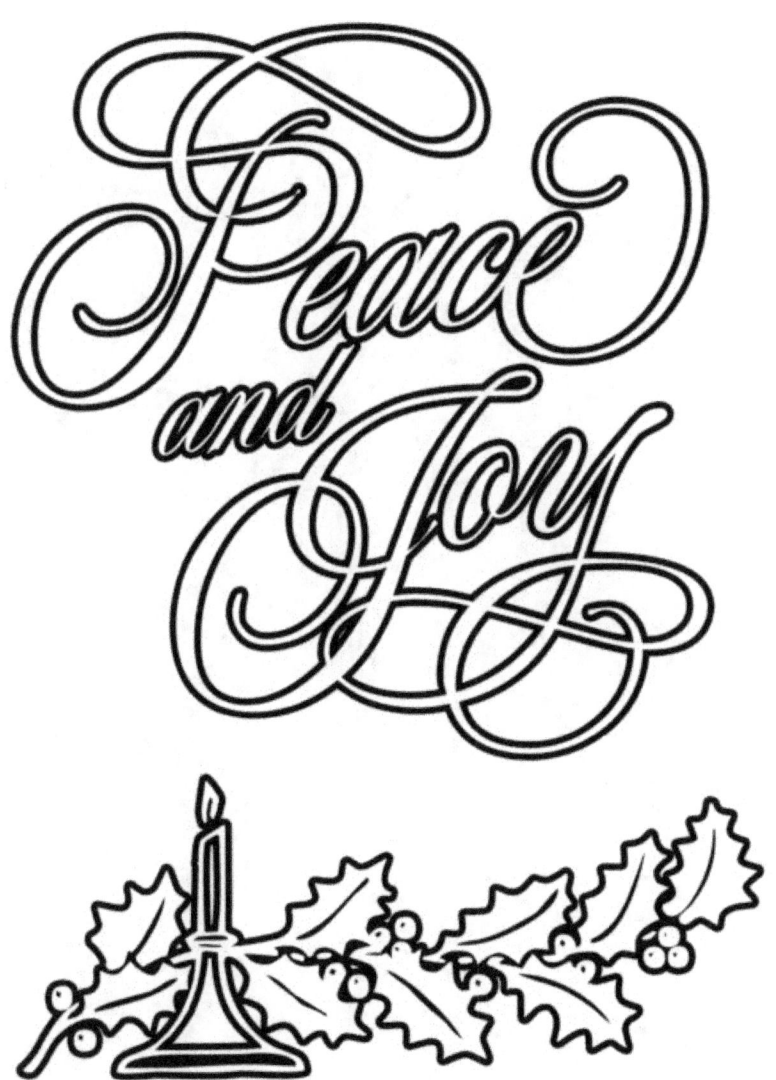

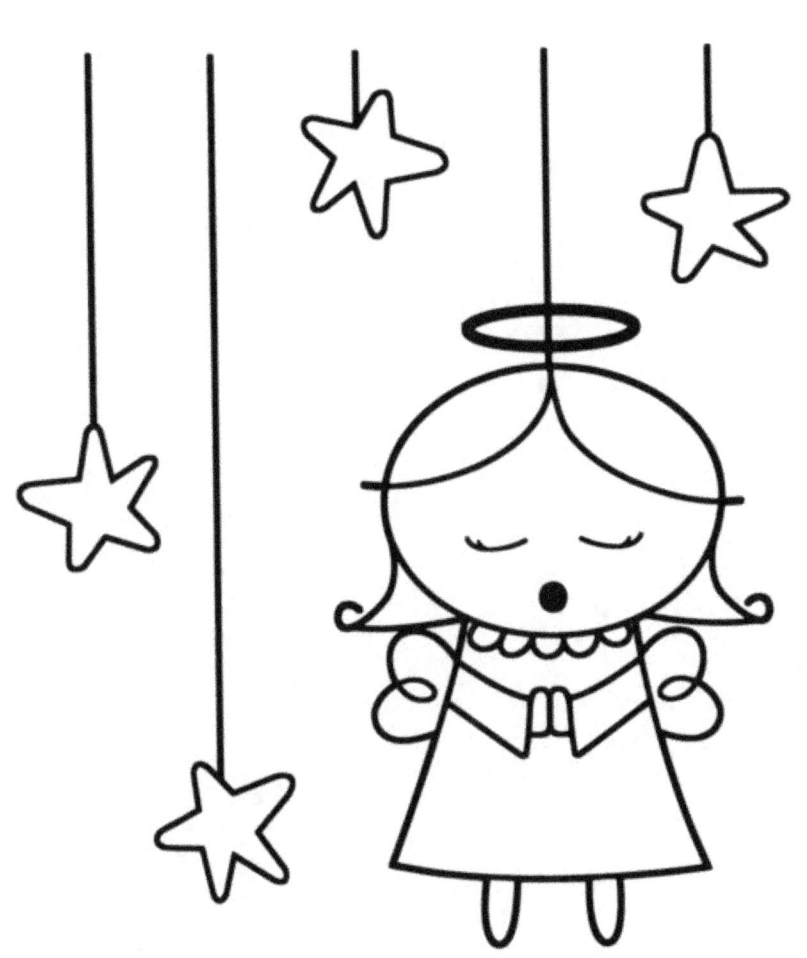

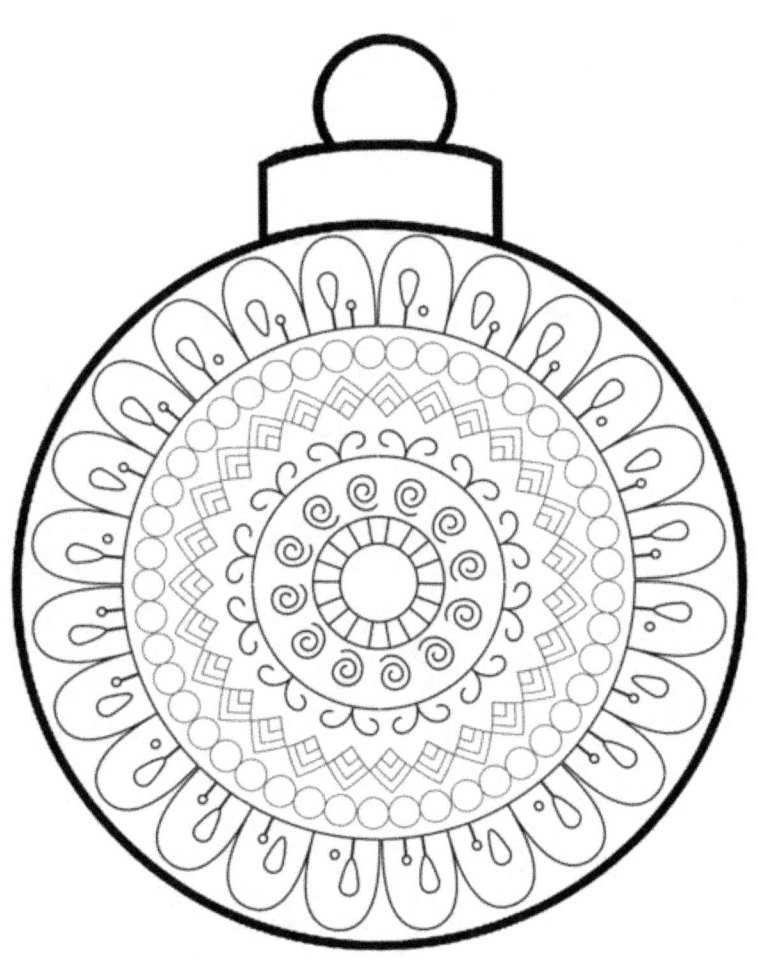

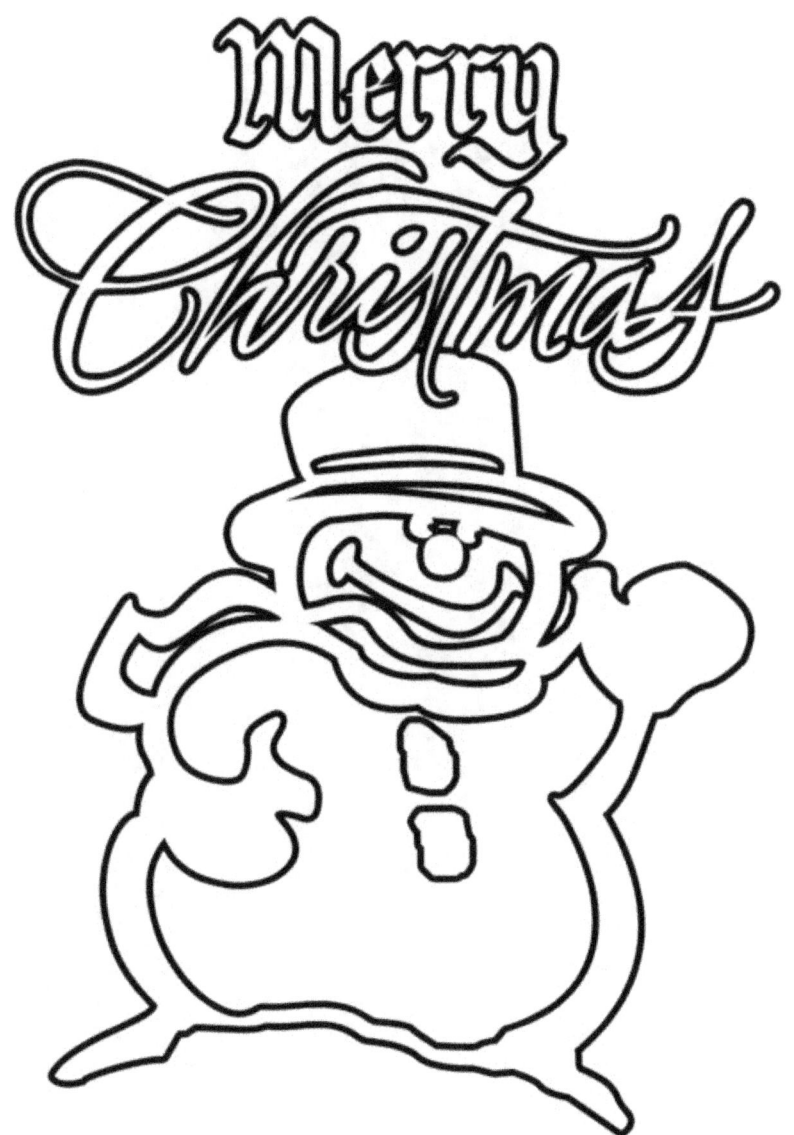

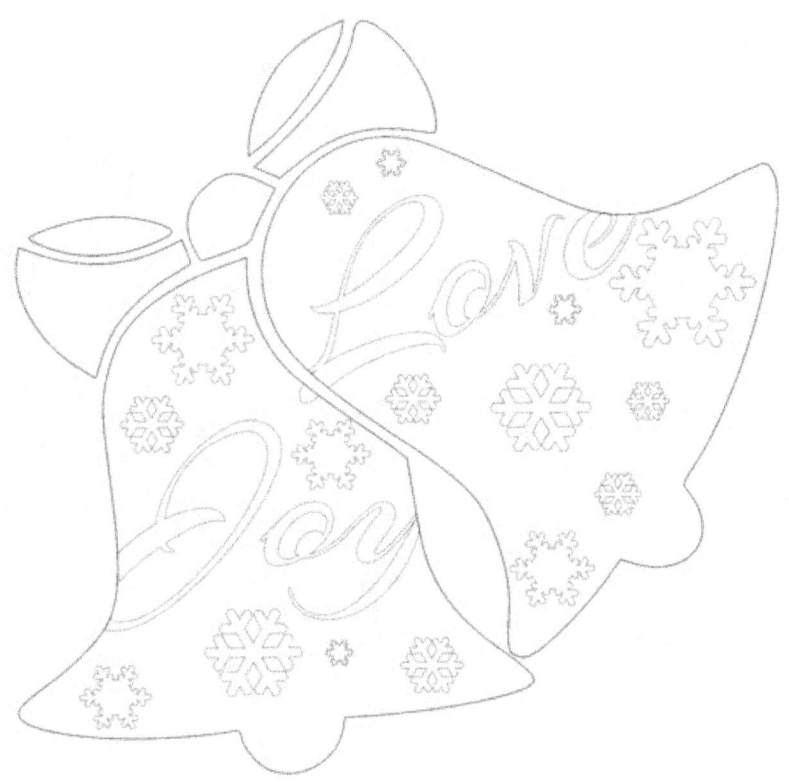

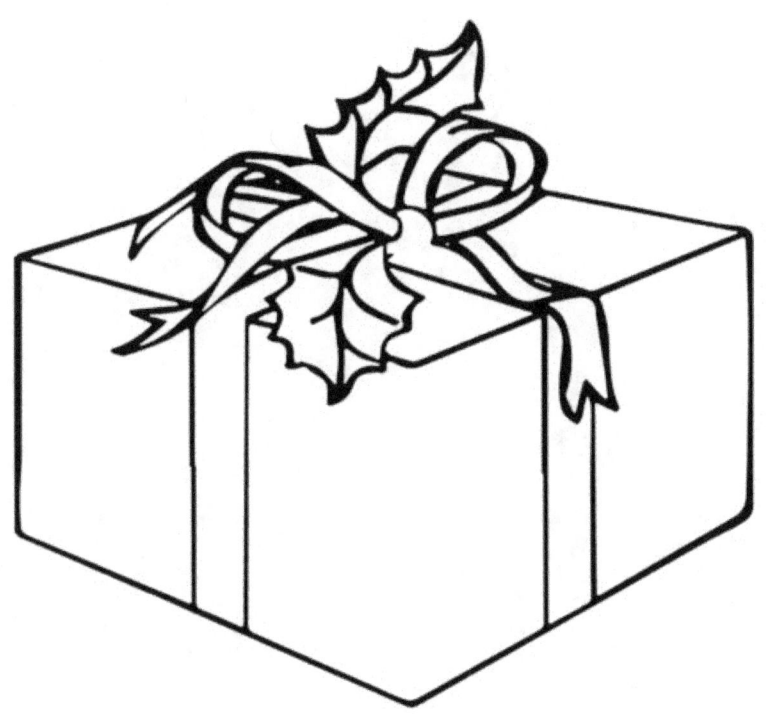

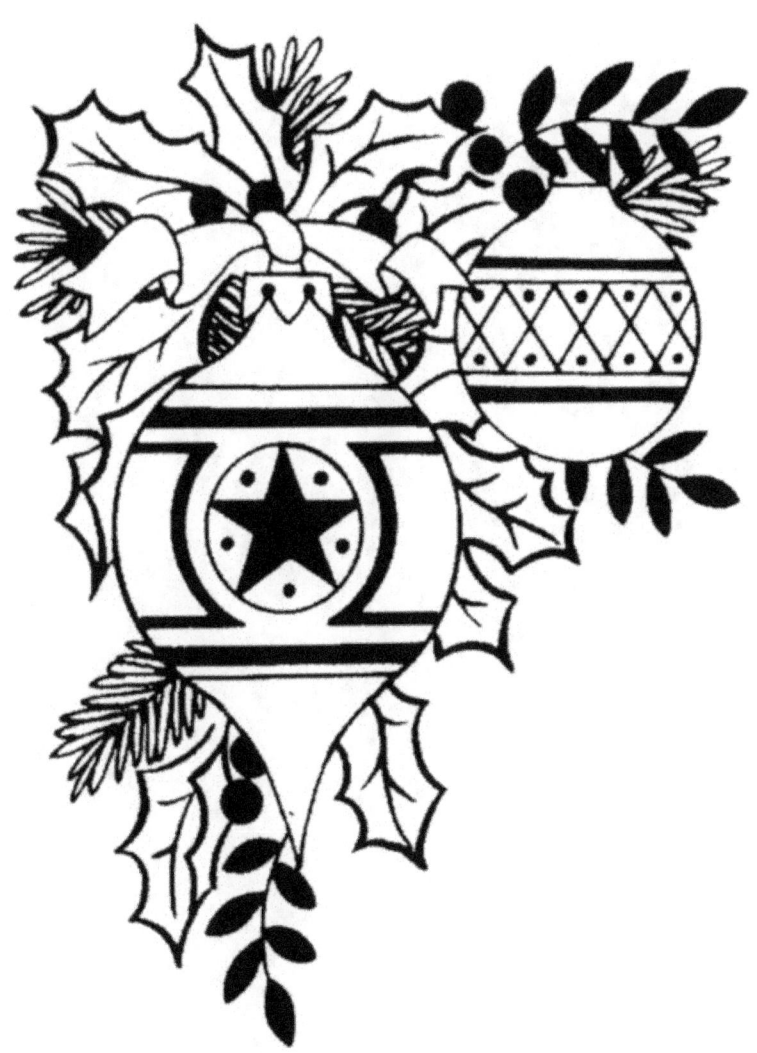

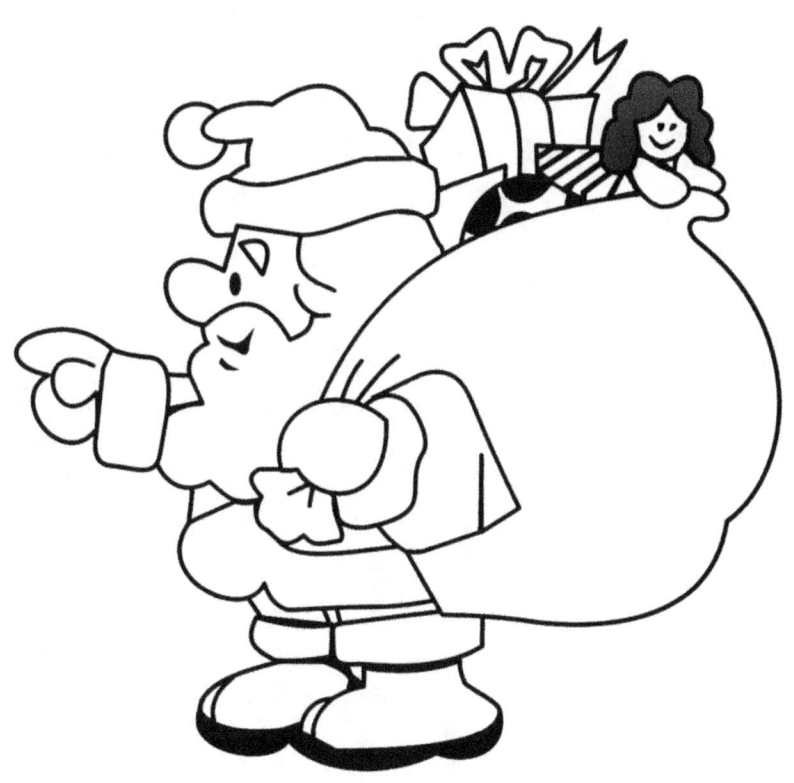

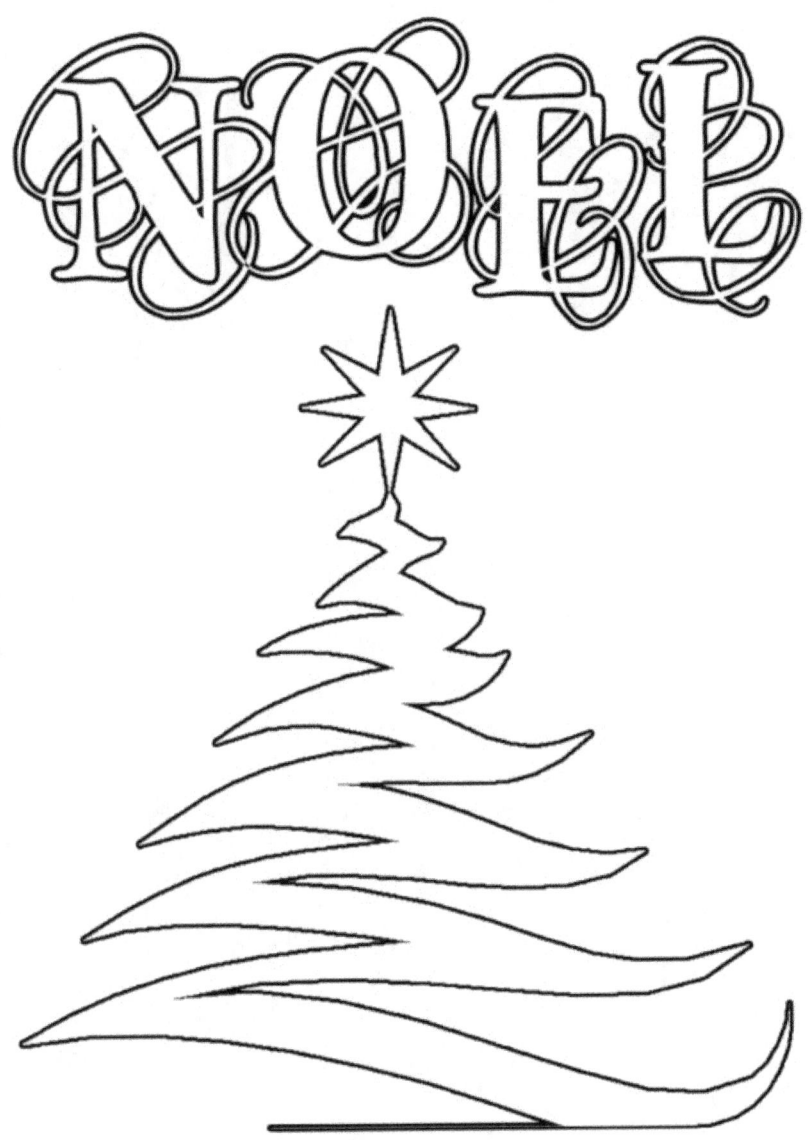

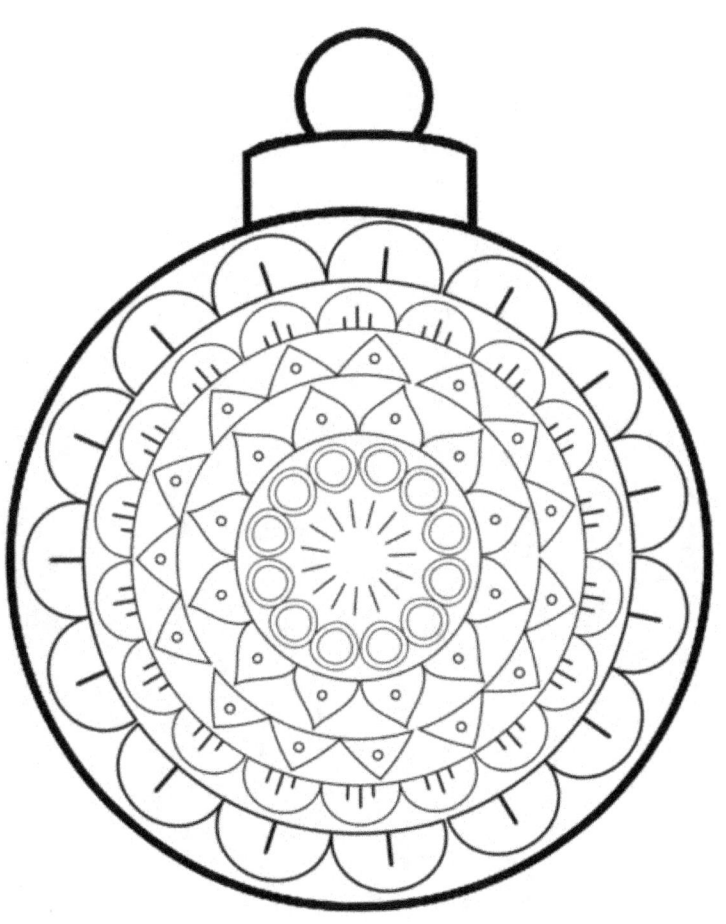

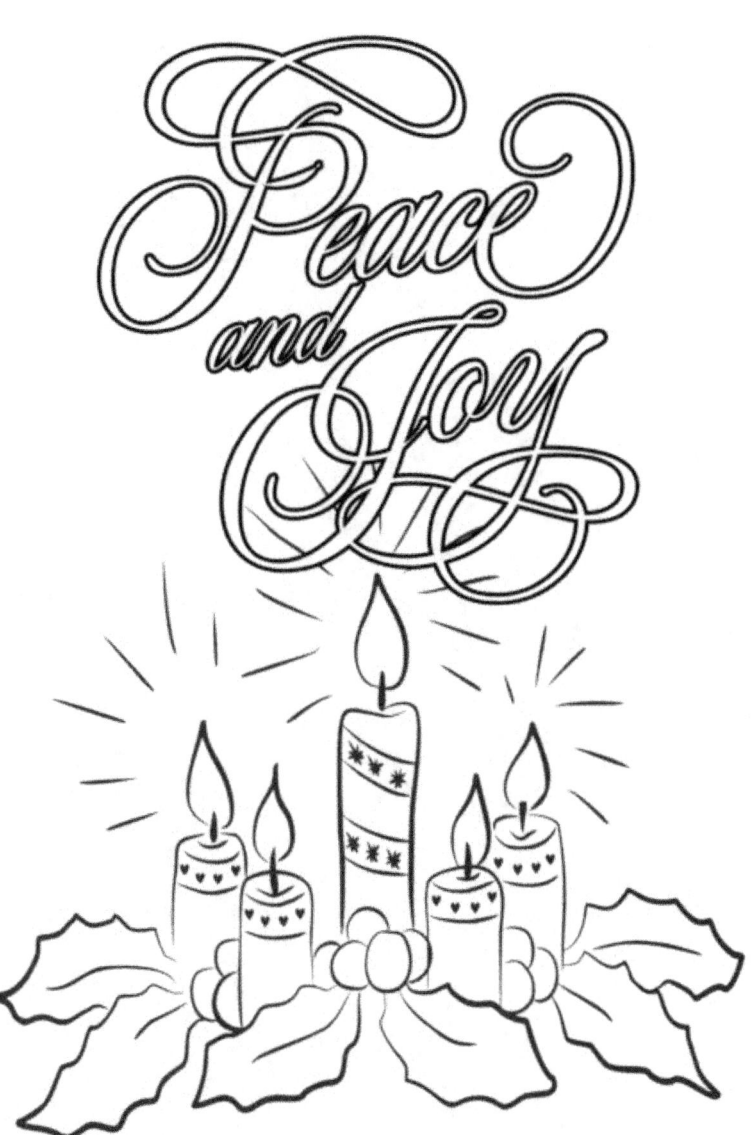

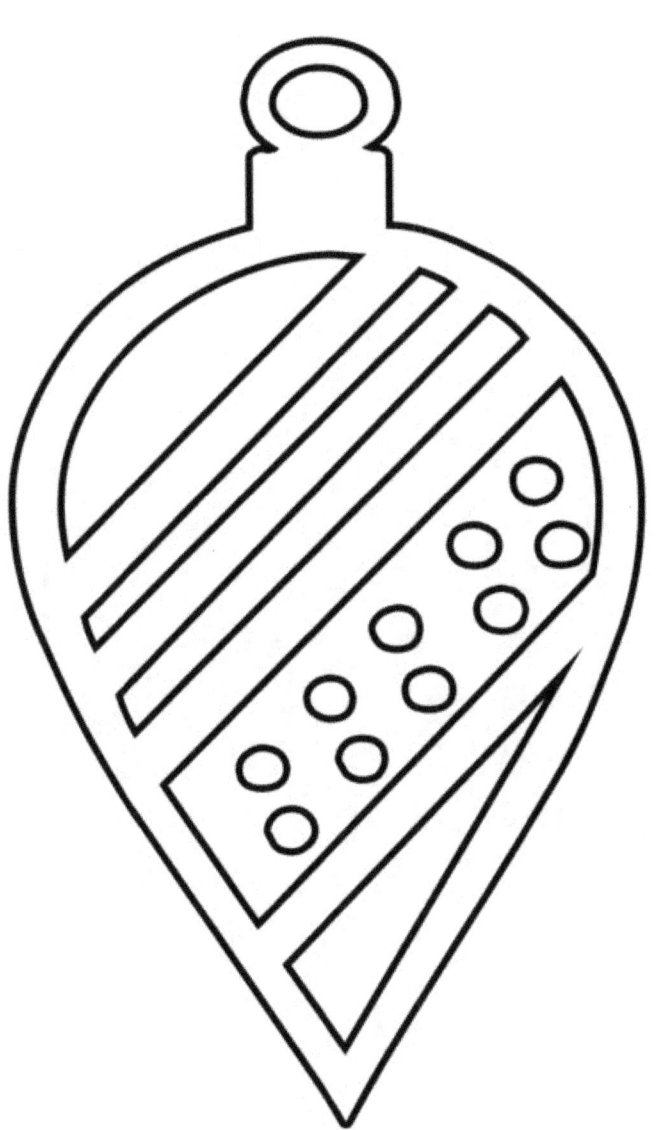

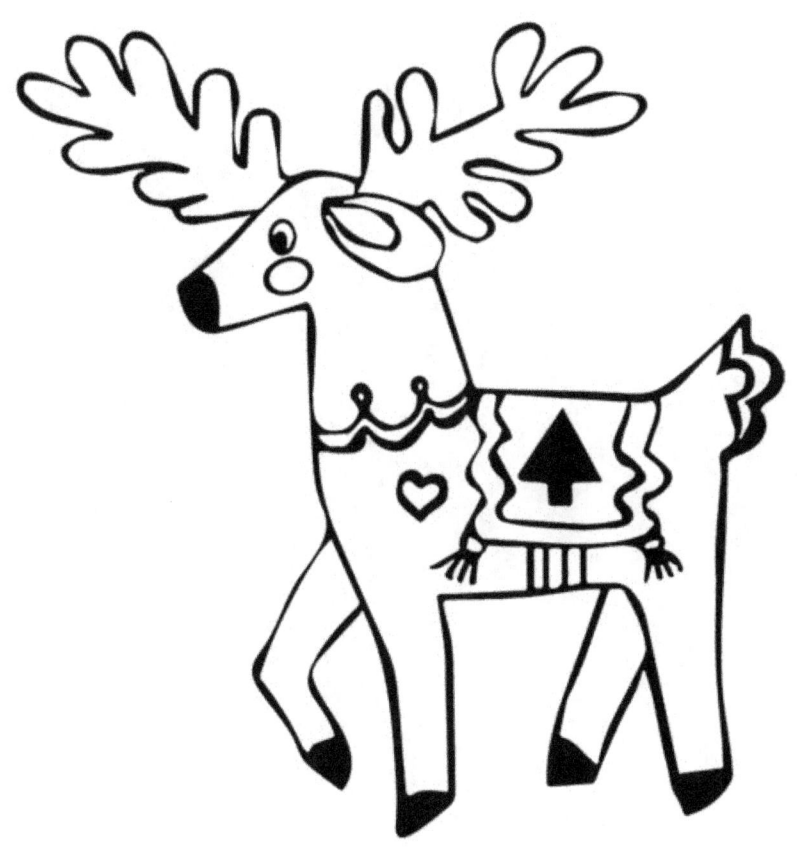

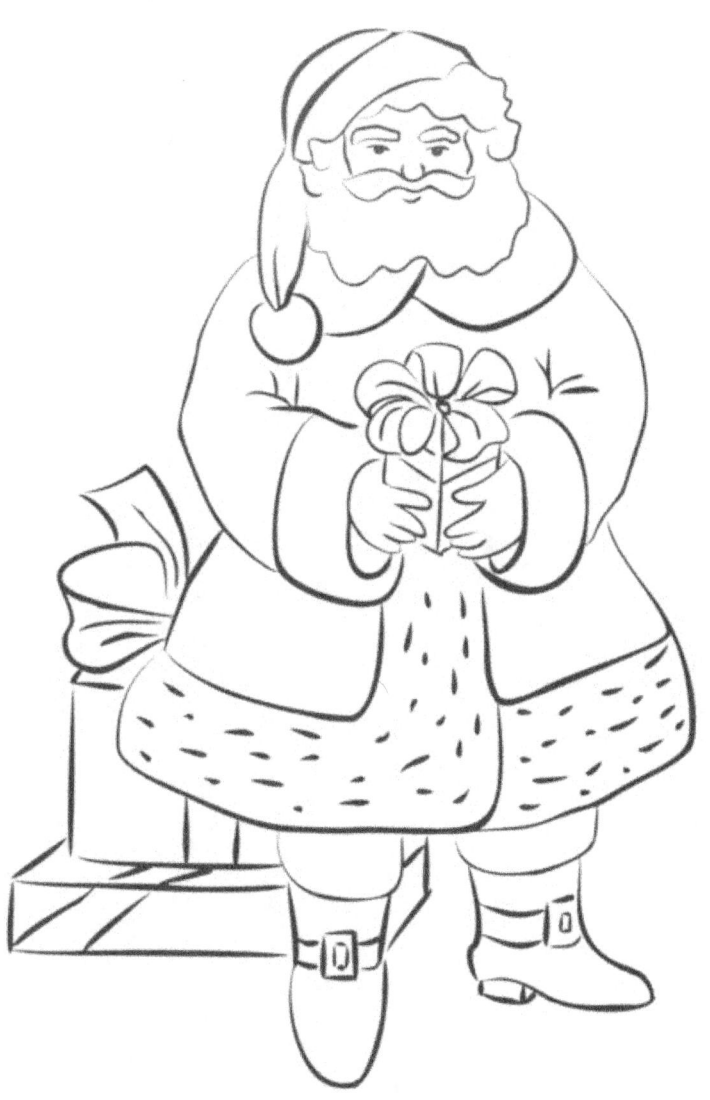

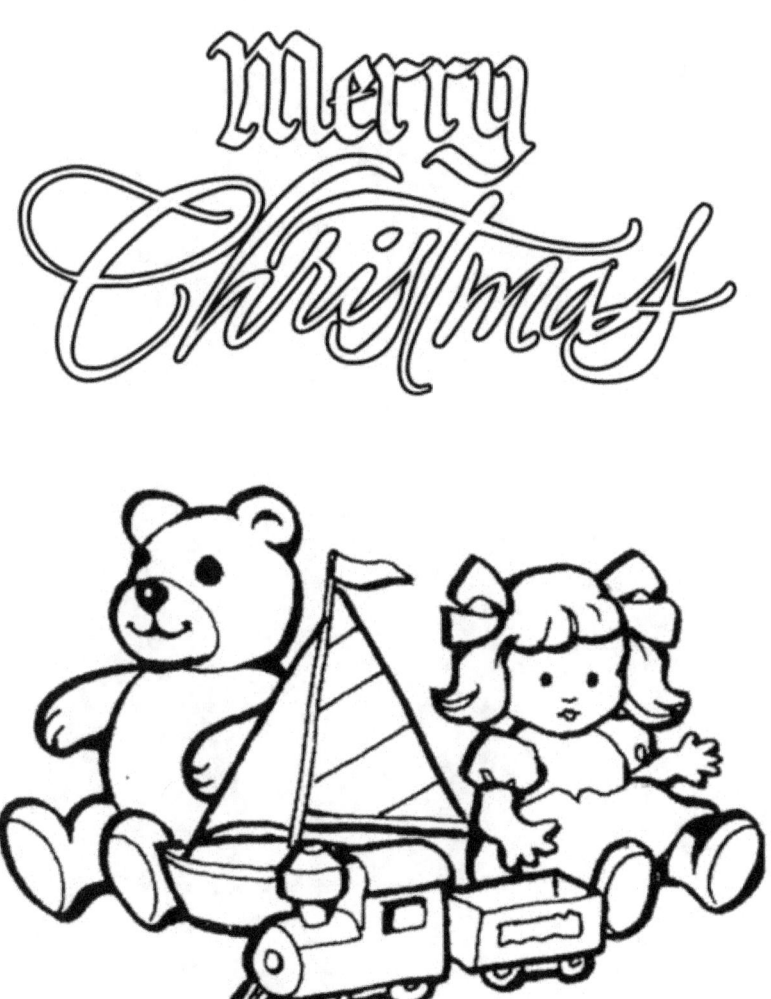

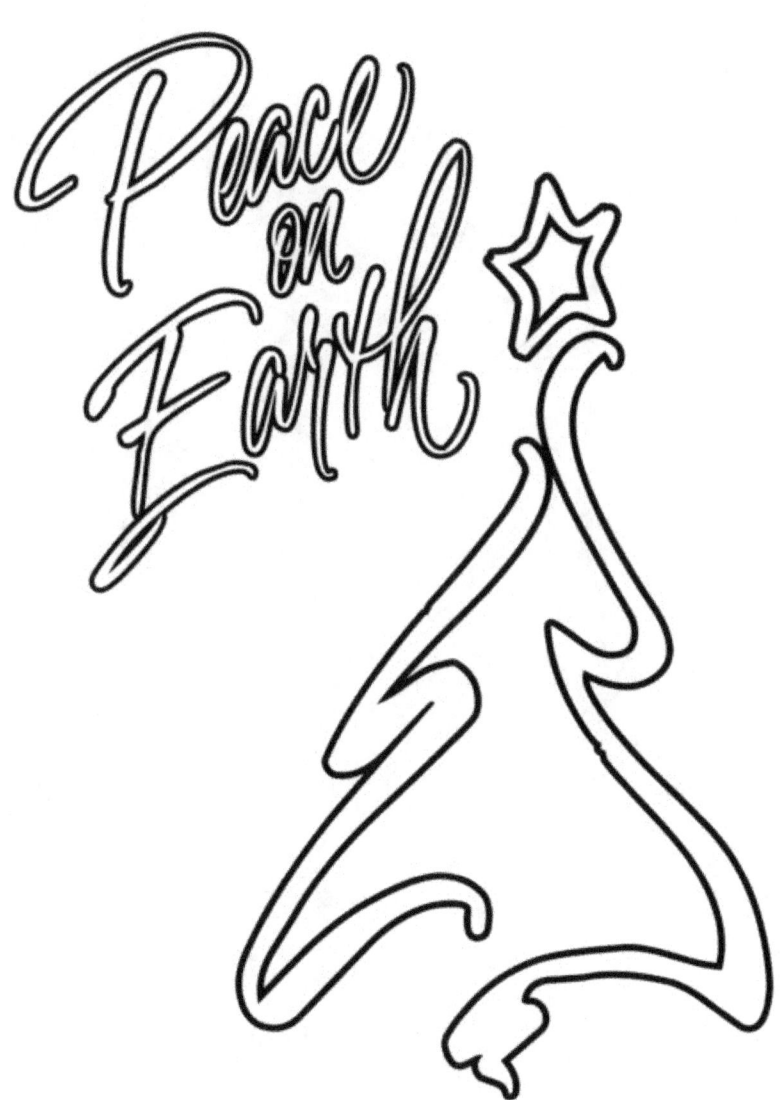

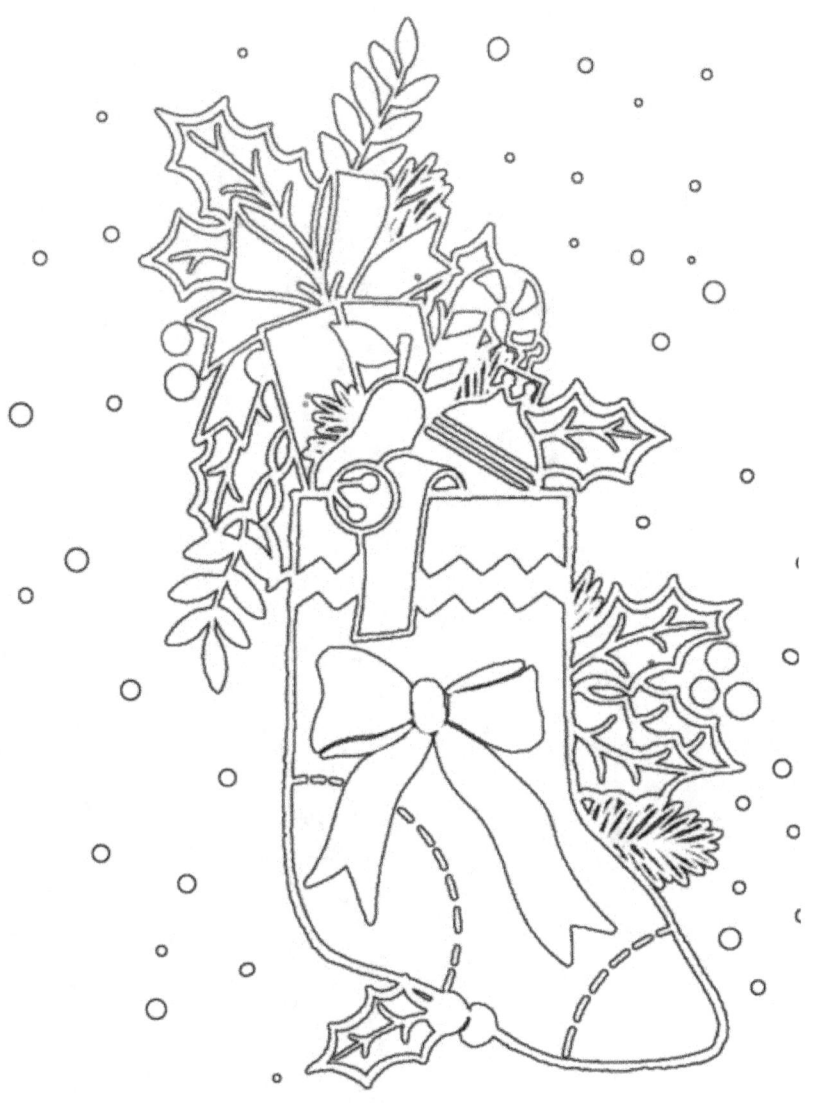

Pocket Pages

Peace
ON EARTH

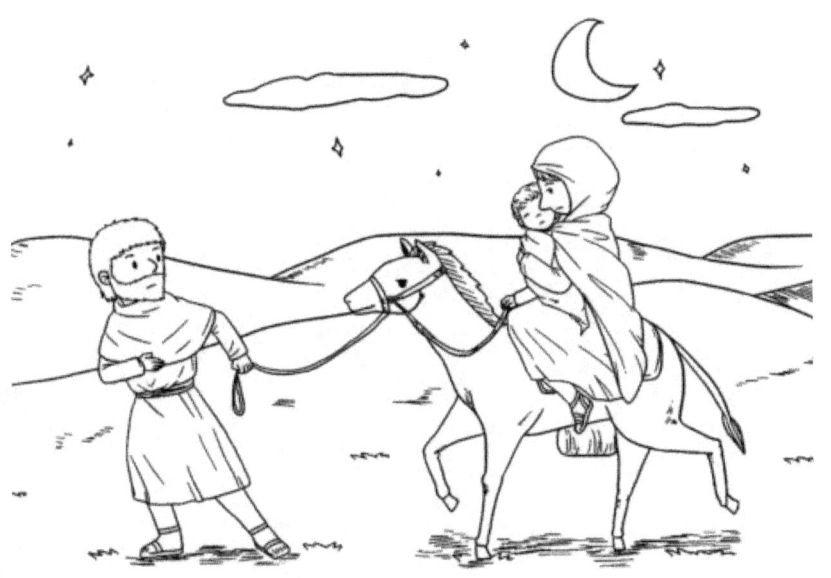

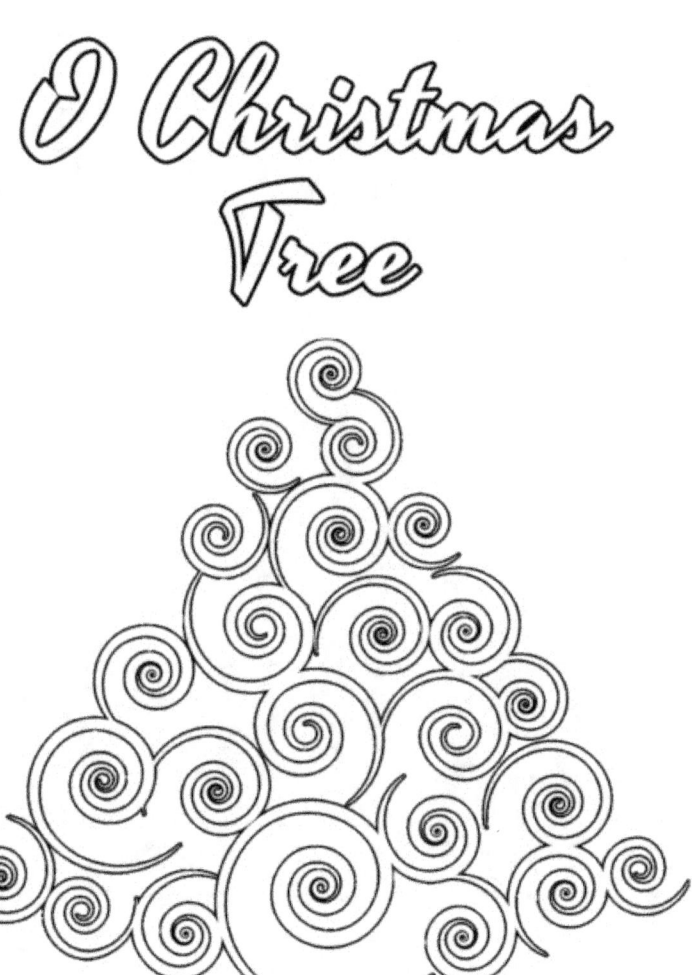

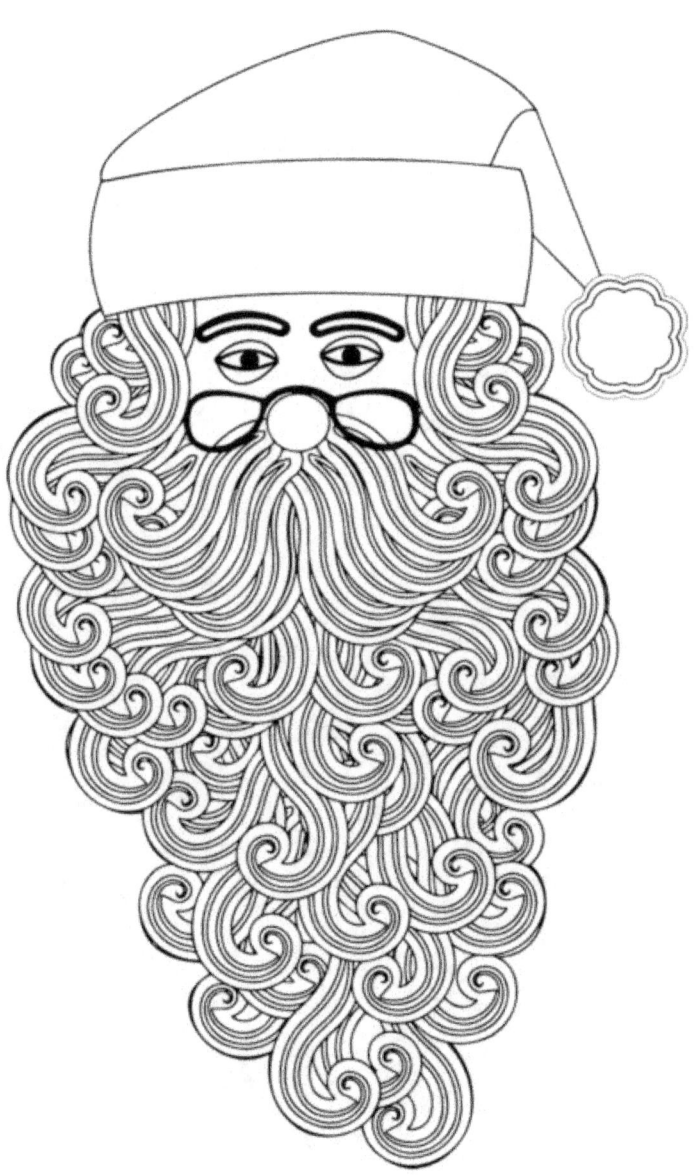

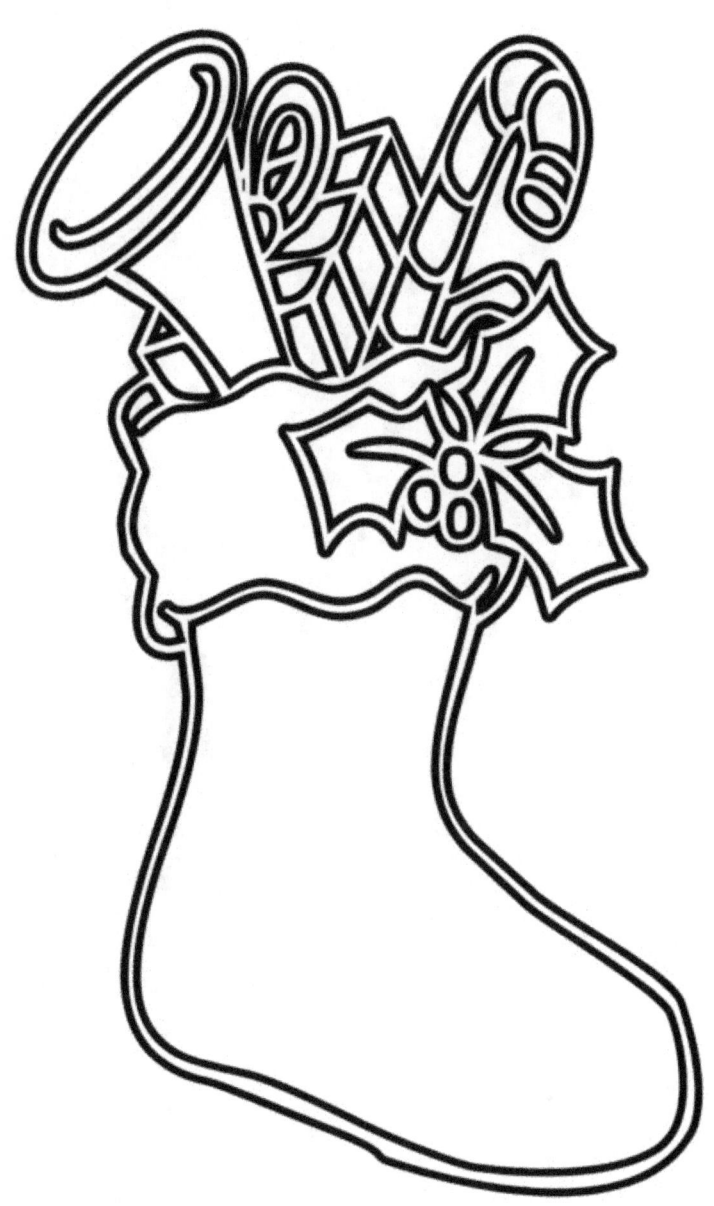

Pocket Pages

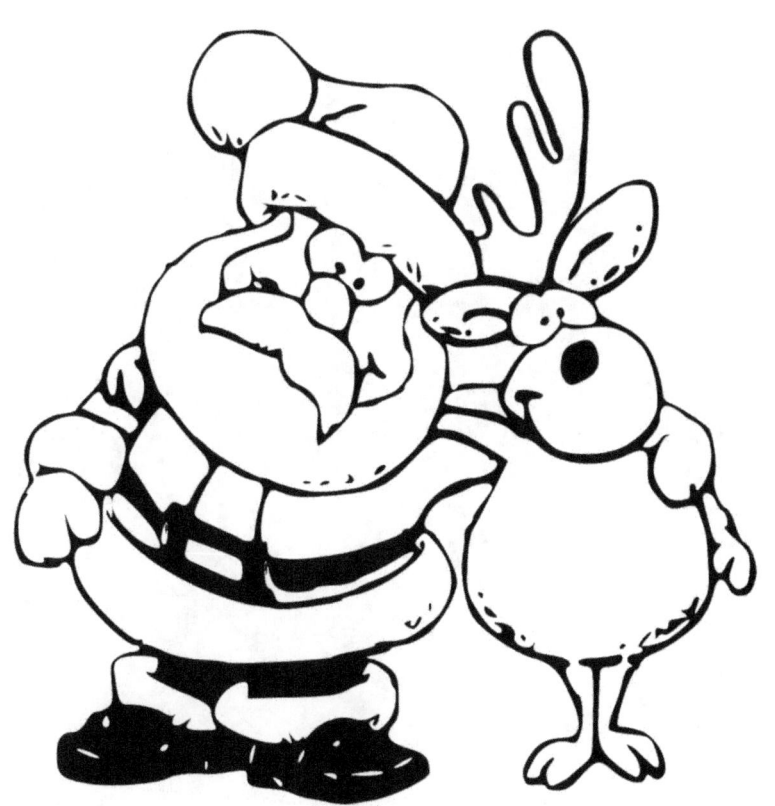

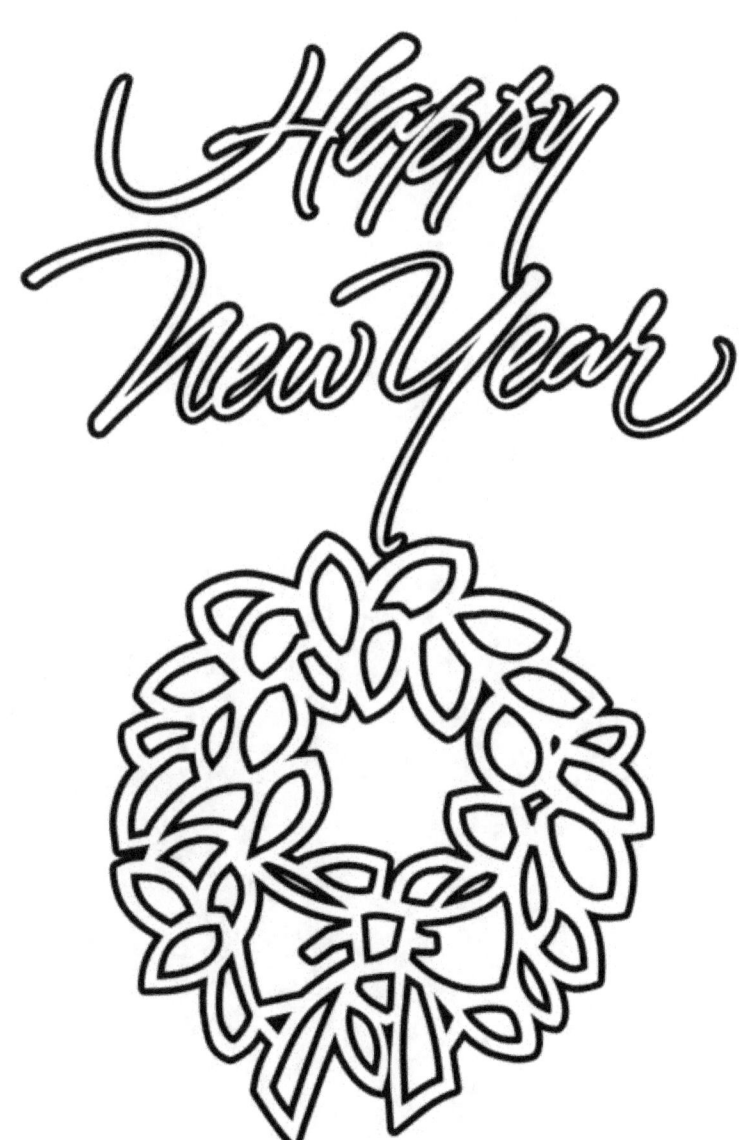

Pocket Pages

www.ingramcontent.com/pod-product-compliance
Lightning Source LLC
Chambersburg PA
CBHW070808220526
45466CB00002B/590